GOD'S CAREER GUIDE

PRACTICAL INSIGHTS FOR THE WORKPLACE CHRISTIAN

PATRICK LAYHEE

Further resources are found at the back of this book.

ISBN 0989481204
ISBN-13: 9780989481205

DEDICATION

To the Christian who gets up and goes to work every day, who wants to do the right things in life, and who wants to serve God along the way. This book is dedicated to you.

INTRODUCTION

God's Career Guide is a handbook for the workplace Christian. Its purpose is to enrich your life by applying God's Word to your career.

God's Word can benefit all workers, everywhere, in all occupations. Work is a high calling from God, and he is the surest source of work-life wisdom.

Work changes, but God never does.

Each God's Career Guide lesson addresses a different aspect of work or the workplace. The lessons can be read in any order, and they are easy to understand.

Parts 1 to 6 comprise six categories: Biblical Principles of Work, Workplace Trials, Fruit and Blessings, Relationships with Others, God's Wisdom and Will, and Work as Ministry. Each part concludes with a summary to serve as a starting point for personal reflection or group discussion. The summaries include key principles, key verses, and several focus questions.

The following verses reflect the spirit of the God's Career Guide message:

Colossians 3:23–24: Whatever you do, work at it with all your heart, as working for the Lord, not for men…It is the Lord Christ you are serving.

Psalm 128:1–2: Blessed are all who fear the Lord, who walk in his ways. You will eat the fruit of your labor; blessings and prosperity will be yours.

Bringing God to work is the best career decision you will ever make.

CONTENTS

Part Two: Workplace Trials   43

Part Three: Fruit and Blessings   85

Part Four: Relationships with Others   139

Contents

PART ONE

BIBLICAL PRINCIPLES
OF WORK

DESIGNED TO WORK

GOD CREATED US, the work we do, and the world in which we perform it.

On creation days one through five, God created water, light, the heavens, the earth, animals, plants, and more. He spoke these things into existence. Then, on day six, God created mankind and gave us his commands on what he wants us to do.

These commands include mankind's original job description as revealed in the following verses from Genesis, chapters one and two:

Genesis 1:26: Then God said, "Let us make man in our image, in our likeness, and let them rule over the fish of the sea and the birds of the air, over the livestock, over all the earth, and over all the creatures that move along the ground."

3

Genesis 1:28: God blessed them and said to them, "Be fruitful and increase in number; fill the earth and subdue it."

Genesis 2:15: The Lord God took the man and put him in the Garden of Eden to work it and take care of it."

Genesis 2:19: He brought them to the man to see what he would name them; and whatever the man called each living creature, that was its name.

"Man" in Genesis 1:26, 2:15, and 2:19 refers to all humankind and is inclusive of male and female.

Consider the five work-related commands contained in the verses:

Rule over

God designed us to take an active role in the use and development of his created order. In our ruling over the things of God, we manage what God created, and we do this in ways that honor him.

Subdue

In the language of the Old Testament, "subdue" means to take control. We are the crown of God's creation, and he gave us dominion over his created order (e.g., the animals, the plants, and the earth).

At this point in human history in the Garden of Eden, there was no sin or disharmony with God. Mankind was obedient to God and only knew to do what was good.

Work

God calls us to work and to serve him with our labor. We are designed to be fulfilled when we are working (i.e., being active, productive, and creative).

The Garden of Eden was never a place of idleness. It was a place where mankind would work, grow, and develop the things of God.

Take care of

We are stewards of what he has given us to rule over, subdue, and work. We watch over and guard God's creation. God still owns it all, and we take care of it on his behalf.

Work is a high calling from God. God has called all of mankind to a life of productive work in the world he created.

Name them

By naming the animals, Adam was demonstrating mankind's God-ordained dominion over the animal kingdom.

The naming of the animals was intellectual work rather than physical labor. Adam was the world's first knowledge worker.

🌿 Begin to see your work as a high calling from God.

LIFE'S THREE PRIORITIES

HAVE YOU DEFINED your life's priorities? Your priorities are what you give special attention to. As a Christian in a world full of choices, what is most important in your life?

Genesis 1 reveals that life's top three priorities are God, family, and work. God gave us these priorities in the Garden of Eden. His words are recorded in Genesis 1:26–28.

> Then God said, "Let us make man in our image, in our likeness, and let them rule over the fish of the sea and the birds of the air, over the livestock, over all the earth, and over all the creatures that move along the ground." So God created man in his own image, in the image of God he created him; male and female he created them. God blessed them and said to them, "Be fruitful and increase in number; fill the earth and subdue it. Rule over the fish

of the sea and the birds of the air and over every living creature that moves on the ground."

God first

God created you in his image and likeness, and you are at your best when you are in fellowship with him.

Today, you manifest the image and likeness of God by being like his Son, Jesus Christ. Hebrews 1:3 says, "The Son is the radiance of God's glory and the exact representation of his being."

Jesus is describing himself in Revelation 22:13 when he declares, "I am the Alpha and the Omega, the First and the Last, the Beginning and the End."

Your first priority in life is your relationship with Jesus Christ.

Then family

"Be fruitful and increase in number; fill the earth." These are God's first spoken words to mankind. They are the Creator's personal instructions to his creation. These words speak to the importance of the family.

The family is mankind's most basic social unit. It is God's idea, and it is sacred. Not everyone is called to marriage and children (1 Cor. 7:8), but everyone is part of a family.

Enjoy, nurture, and protect your family—this is one of your life's most important priorities, second only to your relationship with God.

Then work

Finally, God instructs you to subdue the earth and rule over his creation. You do this through your daily labor in which you are the steward of the things God has given you.

God uses the fruits of your labor to provide for your physical, social, and community needs as well as the needs of others. God is engaged and active throughout all of the world's workplaces.

Your work is Kingdom work.

✎ Get these priorities straight—God, family, and work—and the rest of life will fall into place.

3

CONNECTING GOD WITH WORK

ORK DONE GOD'S way goes beyond coworkers and customers, beyond profit and production. God designed all human work to have a spiritual connection in him. In God's eyes your work is much more than mere secular labor.

Both the Old and New Testaments speak to this spiritual connection between God and your everyday labor.

The Hebrew word *avodah*

Avodah is used in the beginning chapters of Genesis where it is the Hebrew word for "work." Genesis 2:5 reads, "There was no man to work the ground," and a few verses later 2:15 says, "The Lord God took the man and put him in the Garden of Eden to work it." *Avodah* is used again in Genesis 4:2 when God says, "Cain worked the soil."

In Genesis 2:5, 2:15, and 4:2, *avodah* is God's word for "work," but the same word is also translated elsewhere in the Old Testament as *"worship."*

Here are two examples of *avodah* being used to describe not work but worship: Exodus 8:1 says, "This is what the Lord says: Let my people go, so that they may worship me." Psalm 100:2 says, "Worship the Lord with gladness; come before him with joyful songs."

By using the single word *avodah* for both work and worship, God is connecting the realm of work with the realm of worship.

When done God's way, your work and your worship share the same spiritual DNA. Both are God-pleasing acts of divine service. To God *avodah* is *avodah* whether in the context of your workplace, your church, or somewhere else.

Colossians 3:23–24 speaks of working "with all your heart, as working for the Lord."

Whatever you do, work at it with all your heart, as working for the Lord, not for men, since you know that you will receive an inheritance from the Lord as a reward. It is the Lord Christ you are serving.

Your heart is what connects you to God, and it is what sanctifies your work. All work is designed to be God-connected.

Your work is just as much about your connection with God as it is the physical or intellectual activity at the time. For example, you can be just as connected to God when working for a wage serving customers in a restaurant as you can by working as a volunteer in a street kitchen. Your heart and whom you are ultimately "serving" are the keys.

Stay connected to God in whatever vocation you have chosen. The Latin root of *vocation* means to "call" or "summon." Your daily labor is a calling, and you have been summoned by God to honor him with your work-life.

You are already God's employee, and you can serve him every day at your place of employment—no matter where that is or what you are doing.

Have you ever considered quitting your job to be free to serve God full time? The truth is you do not have to quit your job because your everyday work is already God's work.

🌿 All human work has a spiritual component.

4

JESUS'S ORDINARY WORK

JESUS CHRIST WAS FULLY HUMAN, but he never stopped being fully God.

Philippians 2:7 says Jesus "made himself nothing, taking the very nature of a servant, being made in human likeness." God, the second person of the Trinity, made himself into human likeness.

Isaiah 53:2 describes Jesus, the man, as humble in appearance. The verse declares, "He had no beauty or majesty to attract us to him, nothing in his appearance that we should desire him."

No royal embellishments, no self-exaltation, no majesty.

Just like us Jesus was born of a woman (Luke 2:7). He became tired (John 4:6), thirsty (John 19:28), and hungry (Matt. 4:2). He could marvel (Matt. 8:10) and be amazed (Mark 6:6). Jesus wept (John 11:35, Luke 19:41). He lived on earth and was able to die. Jesus was every bit human. He enjoyed his family and lived and worked in his community.

Consider the following two aspects of Jesus's earthly work-life and apply them to your life today.

Jesus did ordinary work.

Like you he was recognized by his occupation. In Mark 6:3 Jesus's neighbors saw him and asked, "Isn't this the carpenter?"

Jesus learned a skill, picked up tools, and made things. He worked alongside others. Jesus worked as an example for you to follow.

First Corinthians 15:49 says, "And just as we have borne the likeness of the earthly man, so shall we bear the likeness of the man from heaven."

To do ordinary, everyday work is to do what Jesus did.

Jesus worked in obedience to his Father.

When giving the Ten Commandments to Moses on Mount Sinai, God says, "Six days you shall labor and do all your work" (Exod. 20:9). As a young man, Jesus worked six days a week in obedience to this command. His labor and work were acts of obedience to his Father. In doing this Jesus validated the significance and dignity of the everyday, ordinary work and the workers who do it.

🌿 To get up and go to work is to follow in the footsteps of Jesus Christ.

5

MAKE TIME TO REST

G OD PUT BOUNDARIES on your work, and he did it for your own good. Work has limits. Both work and rest are creation mandates.

God rested from all his work.

Genesis 2:2 declares, "By the seventh day God had finished the work he had been doing; so on the seventh day he rested from all his work."

Why did our Creator rest? Was he tired? No, God doesn't get tired. He did this to demonstrate the biblical principle of resting after work. God rested as an example for us to follow.

Genesis 2:3 gives us further insight when it says, "God blessed the seventh day and made it holy." As a Christian your rest is blessed and holy.

Your rest is more than simply not working, and it is not mere idleness. The fact is neither work nor rest is complete without God. Your rest, like your work, is God-designed, God-commanded, and God-centric.

God "saw" all that he had made.

Genesis 1:31 tells us what God did after he completed his work on day six and before he began his rest. The verse declares, "God saw all that he had made, and it was very good."

Before resting God saw all that he had made. The word "saw" used in Genesis 1:31 refers to something deeper than just seeing with the eye; it means "to understand and look upon with approval." Before resting God contemplated his finished work and appreciated its worth, and you can do the same with your work.

Finish your work day (and week) by recognizing the value of what you have accomplished. Your good work pleases God, and it should please you too. Make time to rest and to appreciate the worth and scope of your labors.

Jesus told his disciples to rest.

In the New Testament, Jesus speaks of the need to rest in Mark 6:31. In this verse, and after a busy day of ministry, Jesus tells his disciples, "Come with me by yourselves to a quiet place and get some rest."

🌿 Work has limits. Make time to rest.

6

SERVE THE LORD

THE PRINCIPLE OF serving God with your work is demonstrated in Joshua 24, the last chapter of the book of Joshua.

In this chapter the Israelites had just completed their conquest of the Promised Land, and they were ready to possess and use the land that God had given them.

It is at this juncture where Joshua assembles the Israelites and reminds them to "serve the Lord" with their forthcoming labors.

His complete words are recorded in Joshua 24:14–15 in which he uses the word "serve" or its variations six times in just two verses. The Hebrew root of the verb "serve" means to work, to till, or to execute. To serve the Lord is to work and till for the Lord.

> "Now fear the Lord and *serve* him with all faithfulness. Throw away the gods your forefathers worshiped

beyond the River and in Egypt, and *serve* the Lord. But if *serving* the Lord seems undesirable to you, then choose for yourselves this day whom you will *serve*, whether the gods your forefathers *served* beyond the River, or the gods of the Amorites, in whose land you are living. But as for me and my household, we will *serve* the Lord." (emphasis added)

Joshua's message in this passage is for Israel to honor God with the work of making a home for itself in the Promised Land. He instructs Israel to serve its one true God with all faithfulness in its forthcoming labors.

You are a New Testament Christian and not an Old Testament Israelite, but the spirit of this message of staying focused on God and honoring him with your work still applies today.

Joshua's declaration at the end of the Joshua 24:14–15 passage continues to ring true for every Christian: "But as for me and my household, we will serve the Lord."

Serve God with your work while building a better life for yourself and your family. Serve him "with all faithfulness" and not the gods "in whose land you are living."

Finally, consider Ephesians 6:7 written by Paul: Serve wholeheartedly, as if you were serving the Lord, not men.

🕊 Broaden your perspective, look beyond the temporal, and serve the Lord with your work.

7

SPIRIT-FILLED WORK

C AN THE HOLY Spirit help you with your everyday job? The short answer is yes. It is not in God's character to call you to a life of daily labor and then turn his back when you show up at your place of employment.

Christians work like everyone else. But we are set apart from the rest of the world in that the Holy Spirit is dwelling within us and guiding us throughout the day.

Paul is speaking to Christians in 1 Corinthians 6:19 when he says, "Do you not know that your body is a temple of the Holy Spirit?" When you received Jesus Christ at your salvation, you received the Holy Spirit.

Bezalel, the craftsman

The first person the Bible specifically names as being "filled…with the Spirit" is not a prophet, priest, or king but an ordinary person who worked with his hands. His name is Bezalel, and he was a craftsman.

The event is recorded in Exodus 31:1–3:

Then the Lord said to Moses, "See, I have chosen Bezalel...and I have filled him with the Spirit of God, with skill, ability and knowledge in all kinds of crafts."

God anointed Bezalel's work—his physical skills and his mind, his body and his knowledge.

God "filled him with the Spirit...with skill, ability and knowledge in all kinds of crafts." The word "crafts" used in Exodus 31:1–3 is the same word translated as "work" in Exodus 20:9 when God says, "Six days you shall labor and do all your work." In today's culture your craft is what you do to make a living.

The Holy Spirit can fill you and help you do the tasks God calls you to do. In Bezalel's case it was to assist in building the Tabernacle.

Exodus 31:4–5 says the Holy Spirit anointed Bezalel to "Make artistic designs for work in gold, silver and bronze, to cut and set stones, to work in wood, and to engage in all kinds of craftsmanship."

In your case it may be to successfully perform your job so you can provide for yourself or others in a way that honors God. The Holy Spirit can anoint your work whether you are working in a church office, a manufacturing facility, an artist's studio, a hospital, or wherever.

Be filled with the Spirit

In the New Testament, Ephesians 5:18 instructs you and every Christian to be "filled with the Spirit," and 1 Thessalonians 5:19 says, "Do not put out the Spirit's fire."

Finally, the Holy Spirit's work in your life is for the common good and not your personal exaltation. This is made clear in 1 Corinthians 12:7: "Now to each one the manifestation of the Spirit is given for the common good."

The phrase "for the common good" is rendered in other Bible translations as "for the profit of all" and "so we can help each other."

Expect the Holy Spirit to intercede in your work-life in positive ways to help you accomplish the things God calls you to do.

🌿 Ask the Holy Spirit to help you with your job.

8

SLUGGARDS DON'T WORK

PROVERBS 26:13–16 DESCRIBES the sluggard. This word only appears in the book of Proverbs, and it is used exclusively within the context of work. A sluggard is a person who does not work. The sluggard's life is characterized by failure rather than success and poverty rather than abundance.

> The sluggard says, "There is a lion in the road, a fierce lion roaming the streets!" As a door turns on its hinges, so a sluggard turns on his bed. The sluggard buries his hand in the dish; he is too lazy to bring it back to his mouth. The sluggard is wiser in his own eyes than seven men who answer discreetly. (Prov. 26:13–16)

These verses reveal three characteristics of the sluggard.

The sluggard makes excuses for not working.

The "lion in the road" is an imaginary threat that keeps the sluggard from leaving his home. The "lion" doesn't exist—it's a manufactured excuse to avoid work.

The sluggard rejects God's mandate requiring mankind to have a productive work-life.

Careers are demanding and full of uncertainties. Career paths are seldom straight, and there are no guarantees. But these realities should not stop you from getting a job, showing up to work, and achieving success in your life.

The sluggard is lazy.

He "turns on his bed" and "buries his hand in the dish; he is too lazy to bring it back to his mouth." He chooses to be inactive and to not work.

Proverbs 6:9–11 tells us that too much sleep leads to poverty: "How long will you lie there, you sluggard? When will you get up from your sleep?…poverty will come on you like a bandit and scarcity like an armed man."

Proverbs 10:4 says, "Lazy hands make a man poor, but diligent hands bring wealth," and Proverbs 20:13, "Do not love sleep or you will grow poor; stay awake and you will have food to spare."

Sluggards do not do well in life because they are lazy and they sleep too much.

Sluggards think they are "wiser" than the rest of us.

Be the opposite of the sluggard. Proverbs 12:15 declares, "A wise man listens to advice." Learn from other successful people. Grow while in your job and remain teachable.

Finally, Proverbs 6:6–8 has good advice for the sluggard as well as every believer:

Go to the ant, you sluggard; consider its ways and be wise! It has no commander, no overseer or ruler, yet it stores its provisions in summer and gathers its food at harvest.

Sluggards don't work, and as a consequence they live in poverty; but your good work yields provisions and brings a harvest.

🌿 Whatever the sluggard does, do the opposite.

9

LEISURE GOD'S WAY

LEISURE IS THE free time you have after completing your work. Work is important, but it does not define your life. The Christian life is big, full, and multidimensional. It includes work, service, rest, leisure, God, family, friends, community, and more. First Timothy 6:17 declares that God "provides us with everything for our enjoyment."

What does the Bible say about your leisure time?

For starters leisure is similar to rest in that both require a cessation of work. The first mention of rest in the Bible is in Genesis 2:2: "God had finished the work he had been doing; so on the seventh day he rested from all his work."

God rested after he finished his work and you should too. This is God's model: your rest follows your work. God ordained a rhythm in life of repeating cycles of work and rest.

Consider the following seven references to your times of leisure:

Psalm 46:10 instructs you to "Be still, and know that I am God."

"Be still" in the language of the Old Testament means to cease striving, to relax, to slacken from labor, or as we would say today—to simply cease working.

Mark 6:31 tells us that even the work of evangelism is punctuated with times of "quiet" and "rest."

The verse reads, "Then, because so many people were coming and going that they did not even have a chance to eat, he said to them, 'Come with me by yourselves to a quiet place and get some rest.'"

Leviticus 23:3 declares, "The seventh day is a Sabbath of rest, a day of sacred assembly."

Sabbath rest is a celebrating rest. Today, we Christians stop working and gather for Sunday worship to express our reverence and thanksgiving to God.

Esther 9:19 speaks of the Jews setting aside "a day of joy and feasting."

The Hebrew root of "joy" is to leap and spin with gladness, as in the contemporary phrase "jump for joy." Take time away from your work to jump for joy in thanksgiving for God's many blessings.

When speaking of heaven, Zechariah 8:5 states, "The city streets will be filled with boys and girls playing there."

To play is to romp and have fun. The same word for "playing" is rendered as "rejoicing" and "to laugh" in other verses.

Psalm 23:2–3 says, "He makes me lie down in green pastures, he leads me beside quiet waters, he restores my soul."

These verses connect your leisure time with the enjoyment of nature.

Acts 2:42 records the first Christians devoting themselves "to the fellowship, to the breaking of bread."

Rest from your work and enjoy fellowship with your brothers and sisters in Christ.

🌿 Enjoy times of rest, celebration, play, and leisure.

10

NO JOB TOO SMALL

MATTHEW 25:14–30 TELLS the story of a master, his servants, and the property the master entrusted to them. Jesus is the speaker, and the audience is his disciples.

Jesus's words in Matthew 25:14–18 are as follows:

"Again, it will be like a man going on a journey, who called his servants and *entrusted* his property to them. To one he gave five talents of money, to another two talents, and to another one talent, each according to his *ability*. Then he went on his journey. The man who had received the five talents went at once and put his money to work and gained five more. Also, the one with the two talents gained two more. But the man who had received the one talent went off, dug a hole in the ground and hid his master's money." (emphasis added)

In this parable the master represents Jesus, the servants represent us, and the master's talents represent the things God gives us while we are living and working on this side of heaven.

These verses reveal the following principles that apply to your career today:

You have been entrusted with God's property.

Jesus owns everything, and he has temporarily given some of it to you to manage. This includes your natural abilities, both physical and intellectual, and your resources, opportunities, relationships, and possessions.

At its core your work-life is real-time stewardship of God's gifts. Whether you are a trainee or a manager, or your work is small or far-reaching—it's all a gift from God, and he expects you to put it to good use.

God has given according to your ability.

God gives customized gifts. "To one he gave five talents of money, to another two talents, and to another one talent." God's gifts are perfect for who you are today.

In God's eyes and in the context of your career, no job is too small.

Be faithful with what God has given you today, and he will take care of everything else. When you are ready, he will bless you with more and greater things tomorrow. God's plan for you goes far beyond your current position on a company organization chart.

God respects every bit of your good work regardless of its pay, scope, or setting. No job is too small if it is what God has for you today. The world may be telling you that your talents are too few, but God won't agree.

Finally, in Matthew 25:23, the master praises the two faithful servants when he says, "Well done, good and faithful servant! You have been faithful with a few things; I will put you in charge of many things. Come and share your master's happiness!"

"You have been faithful." This is what God wants to say to you and every Christian. He is ready to reward your good work with these words: "Well done, good and faithful servant!... Come and share your master's happiness!"

❧ Do great work regardless of its pay, prestige, or setting.

11

RETIREMENT AND THE BIBLE

S OONER OR LATER most working Christians ask the question, "What does the Bible say about retirement?"

The answer is found in Numbers 8:23–26, which is the only Bible passage referring specifically to this topic. In these verses God is telling Moses that the Levite priests in the Tent of Meeting must retire. The passage reads:

The Lord said to Moses, "This applies to the Levites: Men twenty-five years old or more shall come to take part in the work at the Tent of Meeting, but at the age of fifty, they must retire from their regular service and work no longer. They may assist their brothers in performing their duties at the Tent of Meeting, but they themselves must not do the work."

We are New Testament Christians and are no longer under the law (we don't have to retire "at the age of fifty"), but the wisdom of God's message regarding the cessation of regular work is still valuable and can be helpful to our lives today.

God is saying "they must retire from their regular service and work no longer."

God created work, and your work is his divine calling, but there will come a point in your life when you stop doing regular, full-time work.

The word "work" in this Numbers 8 passage, as in "work no longer," is the same word used to describe mankind's daily labor in Genesis 2:15 which declares, "The Lord God took the man and put him in the Garden of Eden to work it and take care of it."

In the context of Genesis 2:15, the work is Adam and Eve's tilling of the ground in the Garden, and by extension all the various types of labor that will follow. It is these and all occupations (e.g., tilling the ground, serving in the Tent of Meeting, and the daily work of your own career) from which God's people can someday retire.

The retired Levites "may assist their brothers in performing their duties."

To "assist" means to help, to guard, or to attend to others. To retire from regular work opens the door to new and different ways to serve God and others.

As a retiree you can assist, help, guard, and attend to the next generation. This can include your family members, neighbors, or society in general. Whatever form this assistance and help will take in your latter years is between you and God. Remain active, bless others, share, and give.

Also, Psalm 71:18 speaks of the "old and gray," and the "next generation" when it says, "Even when I am old and gray, do not

forsake me, O God, till I declare your power to the next generation, your might to all who are to come."

Do not forsake the Lord when you are "old and gray." Attend
to the "next generation."

Finally, Paul defines the character of older believers in
Titus 2:2–3: "Teach the older men to be temperate, worthy of
respect, self-controlled, and sound in faith, in love and in endurance. Likewise, teach the older women to be reverent in the way
they live."

🖎 Help others during your retirement years.

12

WHY WAS JESUS A CARPENTER?

J ESUS WAS A carpenter by trade. He picked up tools and made things. Jesus learned a craft and worked just like the others in his community.

"Isn't this the carpenter?" some asked in Mark 6:3. Jesus could have worked in another occupation such as physician, priest, scholar, soldier, fisherman, shepherd, or even an earthly king. But why did Jesus choose to be a carpenter?

Jesus, the Builder

Carpenters make things of utility and value. The carpenter does the work, and the object in his hand yields to his design. Carpenters have a plan. They take what is common and make it special.

Carpenters are builders, and this is what God the Father wants us to understand about his Son—Jesus Christ is a builder.

Jesus builds in the natural and the supernatural, in the material and the spiritual. Jesus built the universe. Colossians

1:16–17 tells us Jesus created all things whether "in heaven and on earth...visible or invisible." The passage reads, "For by him all things were created: things in heaven and on earth, visible and invisible, whether thrones or powers or rulers or authorities; all things were created by him and for him. He is before all things, and in him all things hold together."

What Jesus creates, he sustains: "In him all things hold together."

Today, Jesus is building you, me, and every Christian. There is no person who cannot be improved by the work of Jesus Christ in his or her life. We are in his hands and under construction at all times, and his plan is to make us more like him.

Much of Jesus's construction takes place where we spend most of our time, and that is at our jobs and in the workplace. God can use the circumstances and events in your work-life to change you for the better. He is sovereign over your successes and your failures. Jesus can bring good out of every situation you will ever experience.

Paul declares in 2 Timothy 2:15, "Do your best to present yourself to God as one approved, a workman who does not need to be ashamed."

As a Christian you are "as one approved." Jesus saved you and is working in you now so he can work through you later.

🌿 When you show up to work, Jesus shows up to work.

SUMMARY OF PART ONE

Biblical Principles of Work

Key Principles

1. Designed to Work: Work is a high calling from God and it is good. We use, develop, and take care of the things God created. Work is a divinely ordained activity to be performed to the glory of God.

2. Life's Three Priorities: Your priorities are what you give special attention to. Get these three priorities straight—God, family, and work—and the rest of life will fall into place.

3. Connecting God with Work: Stay connected to God in whatever vocation you have chosen. The Latin root of *vocation* means to "call" or "summon." You have been summoned by God to honor him with your job and career.

4. Jesus's Ordinary Work: Jesus worked just like the rest of us, and in doing this he validated the significance and dignity of everyday, ordinary work and the workers who do it. When you get up and go to work, you are following in the footsteps of your Savior, Jesus Christ.

5. Make Time to Rest: God put boundaries on your work, and he did it for your own good. Work has limits. Both work and rest are creation mandates. Include Jesus in your rest just as you do in your work.

6. Serve the Lord: Serve God with your work while you are building a better life for yourself and others. In the words of Joshua, serve God "with all faithfulness" and not the gods "in whose land you are living."

7. Spirit-Filled Work: The Holy Spirit can help you with your everyday job. He will do it to accomplish his purposes, to his glory, and for the common good of all. Embrace the Holy Spirit's presence throughout the work day.

8. Sluggards Don't Work: Sluggards are lazy, and they make excuses for not working. The sluggard's life is characterized by failure rather than success, poverty rather than abundance. Whatever the sluggard does, do the opposite.

9. Leisure God's Way: Leisure is the free time you have after completing your work. This is God's model: your rest follows your work. Enjoy times of rest, celebration, play, and leisure.

10. No Job Too Small: Do great work regardless of its pay, prestige, or setting. God's plan for you goes far beyond your current place on a company organization chart. No job is too small if it is what God has for your today.

11. Retirement and the Bible: Both work and retirement are God-ordained seasons of life. When you retire remain active, bless others, serve, give, and attend to the next generation.

12. Why Was Jesus a Carpenter: Jesus was a carpenter by trade. He picked up tools and made things. Jesus, the carpenter, is a builder. He builds in the natural and the supernatural. He is the Master Carpenter and you are his project.

Key Verses

Genesis 1:26–28: Then God said, "Let us make man in our image, in our likeness, and let them rule over the fish of the sea and the birds of the air, over the livestock, over all the earth, and over all the creatures that move along the ground." So God created man in his own image, in the image of God he created him; male and female he created them. God blessed them and said to them, "Be fruitful and increase in number; fill the earth and subdue it. Rule over the fish of the sea and the birds of the air and over every living creature that moves on the ground."

Genesis 1:31: God saw all that he had made, and it was very good. And there was evening, and there was morning—the sixth day.

Genesis 2:2–3: By the seventh day God had finished the work he had been doing; so on the seventh day he rested from all his work. And God blessed the seventh day and made it holy, because on it he rested from all the work of creating that he had done.

Genesis 2:15: The Lord God took the man and put him in the Garden of Eden to work it and take care of it.

Exodus 31:1–3: Then the Lord said to Moses, "See, I have chosen Bezalel...and I have filled him with the Spirit of God, with skill, ability and knowledge in all kinds of crafts."

Leviticus 23:3: "There are six days when you may work, but the seventh day is a Sabbath of rest, a day of sacred assembly. You are not to do any work; wherever you live, it is a Sabbath to the Lord."

Numbers 8:23–26: The Lord said to Moses, "This applies to the Levites: Men twenty-five years old or more shall come to take part in the work at the Tent of Meeting, but at the age of fifty, they must retire from their regular service and work no longer. They may assist their brothers in performing their duties at the Tent of Meeting, but they themselves must not do the work."

Joshua 24:14–15: "Now fear the Lord and serve him with all faithfulness. Throw away the gods your forefathers worshiped beyond the River and in Egypt, and serve the Lord. But if serving the Lord seems undesirable to you, then choose for yourselves this day whom you will serve, whether the gods your forefathers served beyond the River, or the gods of the Amorites, in whose land you are living. But as for me and my household, we will serve the Lord."

Psalm 71:18: Even when I am old and gray, do not forsake me, O God, till I declare your power to the next generation, your might to all who are to come.

Proverbs 6:9–11: How long will you lie there, you sluggard? When will you get up from your sleep? A little sleep, a little slumber, a little folding of the hands to rest—and poverty will come on you like a bandit and scarcity like an armed man.

Proverbs 10:4: Lazy hands make a man poor, but diligent hands bring wealth.

Proverbs 26:13–16: The sluggard says, "There is a lion in the road, a fierce lion roaming the streets!" As a door turns on its hinges, so a sluggard turns on his bed. The sluggard buries his hand in the dish; he is too lazy to bring it back to his mouth. The sluggard is wiser in his own eyes than seven men who answer discreetly.

Matthew 25:23: "His master replied, 'Well done, good and faithful servant! You have been faithful with a few things; I will put you in charge of many things. Come and share your master's happiness!'"

Mark 6:3a: "Isn't this the carpenter?"

Mark 6:31: Then, because so many people were coming and going that they did not even have a chance to eat, he said to them, "Come with me by yourselves to a quiet place and get some rest."

Ephesians 6:7: Serve wholeheartedly, as if you were serving the Lord, not men."

Colossians 3:23–24: Whatever you do, work at it with all your heart, as working for the Lord, not for men, since you know that you will receive an inheritance from the Lord as a reward. It is the Lord Christ you are serving.

FOCUS QUESTIONS

How many hours do you spend at work and in work-related activities? To what extent is work the dominate activity in your life?

God designed us to work. How can the following action words from Genesis 1 and 2 be applied to your work today: rule over, subdue, work, take care of?

Read Ephesians 6:7 and Colossians 3:23–24. How would your work-life change if you began to see yourself as "working for the Lord, not for men?"

What are some ways you can affirm the good work of others at your place of employment, in your community, or within your family?

Read Genesis 1:26–28. Think about your life's priorities and place them in one of the following three categories: God, family, and work.

Give examples of how our culture affirms workaholic behavior. When does a dedicated worker cross the line and become a workaholic at the expense of life's other priorities?

Much of today's culture ignores the God-connected spiritual aspect of human work. Have you ever bought in to the church-on-Sunday-work-on-Monday mind-set (i.e., separating your spiritual life from your work-life)?

Work has limits. What do you do in your times of rest and leisure? What are some things you can celebrate? What does it mean to include Jesus in your rest?

Read Proverbs 10:4. How have your diligence, persistence, and steady work ethic brought "wealth" into your life?

The Lord filled Bezalel with "the Spirit of God, with skill, ability and knowledge in all kinds of crafts." Is there something in your job that you can ask the Holy Spirit to help you with?

Describe a "small" job you had in the past that prepared you for a bigger job to come.

Is there someone in your workplace with a "small" job and who gets little recognition? What can you do to affirm the good work of this person?

Jesus says in Matthew 25:23, "Well done good and faithful servant." In what ways can Jesus say the same thing about you as a Christian in the workplace?

How is your work a blessing to others?

What does Jesus's choice to be a carpenter tell you about his ministry?

PART TWO

WORKPLACE TRIALS

13

TOIL, THORNS, AND SWEAT

A T THE BEGINNING of human history in the Garden of Eden, Adam and Eve were in harmony with God and his creations. Their work in the Garden was stress-free and productive. In fact God declared in Genesis 1:31 that all of creation, including the realm of human work, was very good.

Sin is the problem.

But sin entered the Garden in Genesis 3, and as a result the dynamics of work changed forever. God's response to mankind's sin is revealed in Genesis 3:17–19:

> "Cursed is the ground because of you; through painful toil you will eat of it all the days of your life. It will produce thorns and thistles for you, and you will eat the plants of the field. By the sweat of your brow you will eat your food."

The post-Eden, work-related effects of original sin (e.g., "Cursed is the ground…painful toil…thorns and thistles… sweat of your brow") are still active today. Frustration, stress, and difficulty are frequent realities for every person who works at a job or owns a business. Your on-the-job trials are the contemporary manifestations of the painful toil, thorns and thistles, and sweat declared in Genesis 3.

Sin is why jobs are stressful, why organizations falter, and why people experience conflict.

Jesus is the solution.

Sin is the problem, and Jesus is the only solution. Jesus's work at Calvary made the way for your redemption and freedom from sin's penalty and power. Salvation through Christ changes every area of life for the better, and this includes your work.

Jesus says in John 8:36, "So if the Son sets you free, you will be free indeed." We Christians are free indeed. With God to lead us, we can successfully live and work in today's fallen world.

He can bring good out of all things, which includes every trial we will ever experience.

God is always for you and never against you. His ways are otherworldly and supernatural. As a Christian experiencing stress in the workplace, you have divine resources the world does not offer.

Romans 8:35 and 8:37 declare, "Who shall separate us from the love of Christ? Shall trouble or hardship or persecution or famine or nakedness or danger or sword?…No, in all these things we are more than conquerors through him who loved us."

The "we" in Romans 8:37 are Christians and "we are more than conquerors" because of Jesus's work in our lives.

🌿 God is always for you and never against you.

14

GOD AND YOUR CAREER TRIALS

T RIALS ARE INEVITABLE. They are part of living in our fallen world. Workplace trials cover the spectrum from the simple to the very serious—some trials are more painful than others.

As a Christian you will never face your trials alone. Your Father is at work in the midst of every trial you will ever experience.

Romans 8:28 declares, "And we know that in all things God works for the good of those who love him, who have been called according to his purpose."

Consider this verse in the following four parts.

"And we know"

You know God because of what he has already done in your life. God has a track record with you, and his part of the relationship is perfect. God always does what he says he will do, and he is always right.

"Know" in the Greek means to understand based on personal experience. It is an intimate and relational knowing and is much deeper than mere head knowledge. To know God is to have personally experienced God.

"That in all things God works for the good"

God promises to work good out of all things, which includes all of your workplace trials, setbacks, and disappointments. You may not foresee how any good can possibly come from a particular situation, but God guarantees he can bring good from it—somehow, somewhere, sometime.

Think about Calvary. The believers on the scene were in despair, but God knew better. At Calvary God took the worst thing that ever happened—Christ crucified—and turned it into the best thing that ever happened—Christ resurrected.

God can do something similar with your trials. He can bring good out of every difficult season or situation you ever experience.

"For those who love him"

This identifies the exclusive recipients of God's promise.

The identifying mark of a Christian is love for God. First John 4:19 says, "We love because he first loved us."

Your love of God is evidenced by your salvation in Jesus Christ. God will dispense his favor to "those who love him," and that includes you.

"Who have been called according to his purpose"

God's plans for you are bigger than the trials you may be facing today. He is sovereign over every aspect of your work day, the good and the bad. God will work through you and your circumstances to accomplish his good purpose for your life.

Proverbs 11:23 declares, "The desire of the righteous ends only in good."

🌿 There is no limit to the good God can bring from your next trial.

TWO FACTS ABOUT
YOUR TRIALS

I n m a r k 6:45–51 Jesus's disciples find themselves in a very serious storm. They were "straining at the oars, because the wind was against them," and they were terrified by their circumstance.

This story reveals two facts every Christian needs to know about trials.

Your obedience to Jesus will sometimes result in an immediate trial with the world.

Consider Mark 6:45–48a:

Immediately Jesus made his disciples get into the boat and go on ahead of him to Bethsaida, while he dismissed the crowd. After leaving them, he went up on a mountainside to pray. When evening came, the boat was in the middle of the lake, and he was alone on land. He saw the disciples straining at the oars, because the wind was against them.

Jesus sent his disciples by boat to Bethsaida, yet their obedience to him resulted in a long night of great trial. The phrase "straining at the oars" coveys severe trouble and torment. These faithful disciples, who were squarely within God's will, were fighting for their lives.

The disciples' serious earthly trial on the lake was the immediate result of their godly obedience to Jesus.

Jesus may wait before delivering you from your trial.

Mark 6:48b-51 continues:

> About the fourth watch of the night he went out to them, walking on the lake. He was about to pass by them, but when they saw him walking on the lake, they thought he was a ghost. They cried out, because they all saw him and were terrified. Immediately he spoke to them and said, "Take courage! It is I. Don't be afraid." Then he climbed into the boat with them, and the wind died down. They were completely amazed.

Many hours passed before Jesus "went out to them." Not only was the storm serious, but Jesus actually waited until "the fourth watch of the night," which is just before dawn, before coming to his disciples' aid.

In fact Jesus "was about to pass by them." He purposefully kept his distance and delayed his intervention until the last moment.

Jesus waited because his disciples had forgotten him and not called on his name. The disciples limited themselves to a natural means of deliverance only, and Jesus respected their decision.

Sometimes Jesus will wait and let you have your way while the world fails you, and he will do this for your own good. But, in the end, he will always be there when you finally turn and call to him.

Jesus amazed his disciples by delivering them in an unexpected and miraculous way. After "walking on the lake," he "climbed into the boat…and the wind died down."

Jesus's words to the disciples in their trial are his same words to you in your trial: "Take courage! It is I. Don't be afraid."

🖋 In times of trial, call on Jesus and expect to be amazed by the things he will do.

16

JOSEPH: FROM SLAVE TO RULER

CAREERS ARE LONG and unpredictable. They begin, and, decades later, they end. In between there is success and growth as well as setbacks, struggles, and an occasional betrayal.

Joseph's life included all of these elements. He went from working as a slave in an Egyptian household to being appointed by Pharaoh as the ruler of all of Egypt.

Joseph, the Betrayed

Joseph's story, recorded in Genesis 37–50, demonstrates what God can do for those who remain upright and faithful despite their unfair treatment by others.

Genesis 37:4 tells us, "When his brothers saw that their father loved [Joseph] more than any of them, they hated him and could not speak a kind word to him."

Joseph was one of Jacob's twelve sons, and, during his teenage years, Joseph's older brothers became jealous of him because their father loved him more. One day while Joseph was tending the flocks, his brothers assaulted him, stripped him, and sold him as a slave to a passing merchant.

Joseph, the Slave

Joseph was taken against his will to Egypt where he was purchased by one of Pharaoh's officials to become a house slave.

Despite the radical change in his station and the betrayal by his brothers, Joseph did not turn away from God. In fact he did the opposite. Joseph drew closer. He remained a righteous man throughout his ordeal, undeterred and godly.

God honored Joseph's faithfulness by blessing his work in his Egyptian master's house.

Genesis 39:2–3 reads, "The Lord was with Joseph and he prospered, and he lived in the house of his Egyptian master… the Lord gave him success in everything he did."

But Joseph's trials were not over. Later, and after he refused her sexual advances, the Egyptian master's wife made a false charge against Joseph. As a result he was arrested and sent to Pharaoh's prison.

Joseph, the Ruler

While Joseph was in prison, God intervened again. Genesis 39:20–21 declares, "But while Joseph was there in the prison, the Lord was with him; he showed him kindness and granted him favor in the eyes of the prison warden."

The "Lord was with Joseph" in his Egyptian master's house (Gen. 39:2), and the "Lord was with him" in Pharaoh's prison (Gen. 39:20).

After a series of God-directed events (Gen. 40–41), Pharaoh released Joseph from prison and appointed him as his second in command over all of Egypt. Joseph went from betrayed brother to slave to national ruler, and all by the providence of God.

In the New Testament, Stephen is speaking of Joseph in Acts 7:9–10 when he says, "God was with him and rescued him from all his troubles."

God's plan from the beginning was to place Joseph in a position of authority in Egypt, and this is exactly what happened. With God's help Joseph overcame all of the man-made obstacles in his path. Joseph consistently aligned with God, and God prevailed as he always does.

God blessed Joseph by intervening in his life, and Joseph responded with respect, loyalty, and obedience.

In the end and through his position as the ruler of all of Egypt, Joseph helped his brothers who had previously betrayed him. Joseph was a righteous man of God through and through, from start to finish.

Like Joseph trust in God when others betray you. Remain faithful despite life's challenges, and you, too, can be the person whom God blesses.

🌿 "He who pursues righteousness and love finds life, prosperity, and honor." (Prov. 21:21)

17

HOW TO BUILD CHARACTER

CHARACTER IS A choice. It transcends education, training, and position. Character can't be downloaded, and you won't get it by reading a book—it is built rather than bestowed.

Martin Luther King, Jr. was speaking of character when he said in *Strength to Love*, "The ultimate measure of a man is not where he stands in moments of comfort and convenience, but where he stands at times of challenge and controversy."

People of character are admired because they consistently do the right things for the right reasons. They do well in life. Character is synonymous with integrity, maturity, and moral wholeness.

The key to building your character is revealed in Romans 5:3–5. These verses were written for the person who has already accepted Jesus Christ and who understands the workings of his grace in times of abundance as well as in times of struggle.

"Not only so, but we also rejoice in our sufferings, because we know that suffering produces perseverance; perseverance, character; and character, hope. And hope does not disappoint us."

These verses reveal that the building of your character begins with God's instruction to "rejoice in our sufferings." The Greek word for "sufferings" used in this passage means "pressings" or "pressure." In the context of work, your sufferings are the extreme pressures of your job.

God is not telling you to be happy because you are suffering at work. Instead, he is telling you to rejoice in the assurance of his grace and provision in the midst of your sufferings. The Amplified Bible translates it this way: "Let us exult and triumph in our troubles."

Exulting God in the heat of your trials will produce perseverance, which is the opposite of coping or resignation. Perseverance is engagement with the expectation of victory. Master your next trial, persevere rather than quit, and triumph rather than fail.

It is your God-trusting perseverance that will ultimately build your character. God guarantees it.

The development of character will be the by-product of facing your trials in the spirit of Romans 5:3—5. Character develops during your trials and not before. This is how Christianity works.

Just as victory requires fighting a battle, the development of your character requires persevering through the battle. God is the author of your character and the object of your hope, and he "does not disappoint."

🌿 Victory requires a battle. Persevere. Don't give up.

18

FOUR KEYS TO EFFECTIVE PRAYER

RAYER IS GOD'S way of bringing change to your life. According to Luke 18:1, we Christians "should always pray and not give up." Ephesians 6:18 tells us to "pray in the Spirit on all occasions with all kinds of prayers and requests," and 1 Thessalonians 5:17 says to "pray continually."

The first mention of prayer in the Bible is in Genesis 4:26: "At that time men began to call on the name of the Lord." This is when God's earliest followers began to distinguish themselves from the rest of the world by proclaiming the "name of the Lord" and inviting him to intercede in their daily lives. You can do the same thing today.

Use the following four keys to improve the effectiveness of your prayer life.

Get right with God.

Begin by trusting in James 5:16 which says, "The prayer of a righteous man is powerful and effective." A righteous person is someone who is in a right relationship with God. The closer you are to God, the more powerful and effective your prayers.

The prophet Isaiah expresses it this way in Isaiah 59:2: "Your iniquities have separated you from your God; your sins have hidden his face from you, so that he will not hear."

Sin stifles prayer. This first key to a more effective prayer life is to get right with God by repenting of your sins.

Pray God's will.

God will only do the things that are consistent with his will. He exists to fulfill his purposes, not yours or anyone else's. Pray for his will in every circumstance.

First John 5:14–15 says, "This is the confidence we have in approaching God: that if we ask anything according to his will, he hears us. And if we know that he hears us—whatever we ask—we know that we have what we asked of him."

The second key is to "ask anything according to his will." If you are not sure of God's will in a given situation, pray, "Thy will be done."

James 4:3 tells us why some prayer requests are not granted: "When you ask, you do not receive, because you ask with wrong motives."

God sees all and knows all, and his motives are pure. Align all your prayer requests with his perfect will.

Keep praying.

In the Sermon on the Mount in Matthew 7:7, Jesus says, "Ask and it will be given to you; seek and you will find; knock and the door will be opened to you."

The tense of the Greek verbs in this verse are instructing you to ask and keep asking, seek and keep seeking, and knock and keep knocking. Note the progression from asking to seeking to knocking. God is telling you to press into him and persevere when you pray.

Psalm 105:4 says, "Look to the Lord and his strength; seek his face always."

Picture a mountain climber pulling himself up with a rope and advancing toward the summit. All of the movement is by the climber—he is pulling himself up and not pulling the summit down. This is a metaphor for your prayer life. Prayer pulls you up, moves you closer to God, and prepares you for his answer.

Prayer changes you, not God.

Believe in God's answer.

This final key is to believe in God for his answer that is sure to come.

Jesus declares this fact in the following two gospel passages.

Matthew 21:22: "If you believe, you will receive whatever you ask for in prayer."

Mark 11:24: "Therefore I tell you, whatever you ask for in prayer, believe that you have received it, and it will be yours."

Charles Stanley, teacher and pastor, says God has the following four answers to your prayers: yes, no, wait, or in the words of 2 Corinthians 12:9, "My grace is sufficient for you."

God is your good Father and he will always do what is best for you in response to your prayers.

🌿 "Pray continually." (1 Thess. 5:17)

19

TODAY'S GOLIATHS

GOLIATH WAS A well-equipped warrior who intimidated the people of God. The old Goliath is gone, slain by David, but the spirit of his type of attack continues to thrive, especially in today's workplace.

David faced his Goliath and won, and you can do the same. The following four excerpts from 1 Samuel 17 describe Goliath's methods as well as the keys to David's victory.

Today's Goliaths will bring a fight to you.

"Now the Philistines gathered their forces for war and assembled at Socoh in Judah…A champion named Goliath… came out of the Philistine camp" (1 Sam. 17:1, 4).

Goliath and the Philistines invaded Judah. They were interlopers who waged war on God and his people. Today's Goliaths will do the same. They are adversarial and unrepentant, and they will bring a fight to you.

You and your Lord Jesus Christ are the targets. Jesus says in John 15:18, "If the world hates you, keep in mind that it hated me first." Being the target of a modern day Goliath confirms the effectiveness of your Christian witness to others.

Today's Goliaths will try to control you through fear.

"On hearing the Philistine's words, Saul and all the Israelites were dismayed and terrified....When the Israelites saw the man, they all ran from him in great fear" (1 Sam. 17:11, 24).

Goliaths are bullies. Saul and the Israelites were "dismayed and terrified," and they cowered before their Goliath. Goliaths wield power, flex their muscles, and shout commands. If your Goliath is your supervisor, don't cower or run. Keep doing your job; do it with excellence and to the glory of God.

Today's Goliaths will expect you to fight their way.

"Then Saul dressed David in his own tunic. He put a coat of armor on him and a bronze helmet on his head. David fastened on his sword over the tunic and tried walking around, because he was not used to them. 'I cannot go in these,' he said to Saul, 'because I am not used to them.' So he took them off" (1 Sam. 17:38–39).

David rejected man's conventional wisdom and took off Saul's armor. David responded on his terms and with his methods, not Saul's or Goliath's. Take the high road when facing your Goliaths, and don't stoop to their low tactics.

Take God's side in the battle.

"David said to the Philistine, 'You come against me with sword and spear and javelin, but I come against you in the name of the Lord Almighty, the God of the armies of Israel, whom you have defied. This day the Lord will hand you over to me, and I'll strike you down and cut off your head'" (1 Sam. 17:45–46).

The key to David's victory becomes clear when he declares, "I come against you in the name of the Lord Almighty." To invoke the "name of the Lord" is to invoke the authority of the Lord. Make David's strategy your strategy. Take God's side in your battles.

In the end 1 Samuel 17:50 tells us, "David triumphed over the Philistine." God is stronger than all of the world's Goliaths, and his victories are perfect.

🌿 Take God's side in your battles.

20

DEALING WITH
EXTREME STRESS

I F   Y O U   W O R K for a living, you are no stranger to stress.
Performance demands, conflicts, deadlines, fatigue, and
work/life balance are common stress triggers that are a
part of almost every job.

Paul's extreme stress

In 2 Corinthians 1:8–9, Paul is speaking to Christians when
he describes the extreme stress he and his companions endured
on one of their mission trips, and then Paul tells us why God lets
this level of stress come into our lives.

> We do not want you to be uninformed, brothers, about
> the hardships we suffered in the province of Asia. We
> were under great pressure, far beyond our ability to
> endure, so that we despaired even of life. Indeed, in our

hearts we felt the sentence of death. But this happened that we might not rely on ourselves but on God.

Paul does not want us to be uninformed about the types of pressures we can experience (i.e., the hardships we suffered, under great pressure, far beyond our ability to endure, despaired, and felt the sentence of death). What Paul describes here is extreme by any measure. His trials went far beyond what most of us will ever face in our careers.

Second Corinthians 1:8–9 makes it clear that God allows Christians, even "good" Christians like Paul, to experience extreme stress. This fact is our reality today, and always will be so long as we live on this side of heaven.

Christians are not immune to hardship. But how we deal with our hardship sets us apart from the rest of the world.

Paul learned to rely on God.

At the end of the 2 Corinthians 1:8–9 passage, Paul tells us, "This happened that we might not rely on ourselves but on God." From time to time, there will be stressful situations we cannot handle on our own. At these times—and this is Paul's key point—we are to "not rely on ourselves but on God."

Christianity is not a stress-free life, but it is the best life. Paul never gave up in the face of life's difficulties, and you shouldn't, either.

Psalm 46:1–2 declares, "God is our refuge and strength, an ever-present help in trouble. Therefore we will not fear, though the earth give way and the mountains fall into the heart of the sea."

🌿 With God's help you can handle any stressful situation that comes your way.

21

FOUR REASONS WHY GOD DELAYS

HAVE YOU ASKED God for something—a job, a pay raise, or the resolution to a problem—but his answer has yet to come? Even if you asked with the right motives, are you still waiting for God to act? David expresses this sentiment in Psalm 69:17 when he calls out to God: "Answer me quickly, for I am in trouble."

God always has good reasons for delaying. Consider the following four:

God delays because his ways are not your ways.

"For my thoughts are not your thoughts, neither are your ways my ways declares the Lord. As the heavens are higher than the earth, so are my ways higher than your ways and my thoughts than your thoughts" (Isa. 55:8–9).

God's ways are "higher." Trust that he has a divine purpose for his delay. Your viewpoint is limited, but God sees all things. Proverbs 3:5 says, "Trust in the Lord with all your heart and lean not on your own understanding." God may be putting everything in place before revealing his answer to you.

God delays so you can demonstrate your faith.

Galatians 6:9 tells you how to wait for God: "Let us not become weary in doing good, for at the proper time we will reap a harvest if we do not give up."

Do good and "do not give up." Respond to God's delay with faith, not doubt. God guarantees a harvest, and it will arrive at the "proper time."

Hebrews 10:36 says, "You need to persevere so that when you have done the will of God, you will receive what he has promised."

To persevere is to endure with an expectation of victory.

God delays so he can bless your waiting.

Isaiah 30:18 promises, "Yet the Lord longs to be gracious to you; he rises to show you compassion. For the Lord is a God of justice. Blessed are all who wait for him!"

Those who wait for God will be blessed by God. God will take care of you and show you his compassion while you are waiting for him. He will be gracious, which conveys the word picture of God descending from above to personally show you his kindness.

God delays so he can be glorified in the end.

John 11:4 says, "When he heard this, Jesus said, 'This sickness will not end in death. No, it is for God's glory so that God's Son may be glorified through it.'"

This verse is part of a broader passage in John 11:1–43 concerning the death and resurrection of Lazarus. When Lazarus was sick, Jesus purposefully delayed in going to him. During the delay Lazarus died. Jesus ultimately resurrected Lazarus, which was a manifestation of Jesus's glory for all to see.

Christians are still talking about this miracle today. God's miracles validate his Word.

In John 11:40, at the end of the Lazarus story, Jesus says, "Did I not tell you that if you believed, you would see the glory of God?"

🌿 God's delay is not his denial.

22

THE BELIEVER'S SIFTING

PETER WAS A good Christian—confident, fruitful, and strong. Yet, at the end of the Last Supper, Jesus warned him saying, "Satan has asked to sift you as wheat."

Jesus's full words are recorded in Luke 22:31–32: "Simon, Simon, Satan has asked to sift you as wheat. But I have prayed for you, Simon, that your faith may not fail. And when you have turned back, strengthen your brothers."

To "sift you as wheat" is a metaphor for a trial of faith. When wheat is sifted, the chaff and other impurities fall to the ground while the desired end product, the good wheat, remains in the sieve.

We believers are the wheat that remains and not the chaff that falls to the ground. When God sifts us through our post-salvation trials, we become like the good wheat: cleaner, more valuable, and ready for use. The sifting process makes us better, stronger, and more like Jesus Christ.

Consider the following three aspects of the believer's sifting from the Luke 22:31–32 passage:

Jesus used Satan to do the sifting.

This may seem strange, but it is true. Satan "asked to sift" Peter, and Jesus agreed. God allows Satan to afflict believers, but he limits Satan's influence and reach. Even a "good" Christian like Peter was not immune to Satan's assault.

Satan's goal is to use a trial to destroy your faith, but Jesus's goal is to use the same trial to strengthen your faith.

Jesus prayed for Peter's faith to increase and not for the sifting to stop.

Demonstrating your faith during a period of struggle, regardless of its source, is the bigger issue. In Luke 8:25 Jesus asks his disciples and every Christian, "Where is your faith?"

Jesus promises us in Matthew 17:20, "I tell you the truth, if you have faith as small as a mustard seed, you can say to this mountain, 'Move from here to there' and it will move. Nothing will be impossible for you."

Respond to your trial of faith by magnifying God and not Satan or the trial. Hebrews 11:1 declares, "Now faith is being sure of what we hope for and certain of what we do not see." Every Christian can trust in the intercessory power of Christ.

The sifting would equip Peter to strengthen others.

Who better to strengthen a brother or sister in Christ in a trial than a fellow believer who has come through the very same trial?

First Thessalonians 5:11–14 says, "Therefore encourage one another and build each other up…respect those who work hard among you…encourage the timid, help the weak."

Just as the sifting process brings forth the best of the wheat, a trial of faith can bring forth the best in you. Learn something new and become stronger as a result of every trial you ever experience.

🌿 Trust in the intercessory power of Christ.

23

TRIALS AS TRAINING

T HE WORKPLACE IS no Garden of Eden. While it is a place where God can bless and reward you, it is also rife with frustration and stress.

Trials take their toll on every conscientious worker, believers and unbelievers alike. However, and for the believer, God can use each on-the-job trial as a means to build you up rather than break you down.

Hebrews 12:5–11 speaks to this issue, and verses 7 and 11 are a good summary of the passage.

Hebrews 12:7: "Endure hardship as discipline; God is treating you as sons."

If you let him, God will use your trials to get your attention about things you would not address otherwise. He will guide you through your trials and teach you new things in the process.

"Discipline" in the Greek means to train, educate, or instruct. God's discipline of his followers is consistent with the actions of loving parents who are training their child. The parents' training is purposeful and measured. The parents always have their child's best interest in mind, even when the child does not understand their good intentions.

God's discipline of his children via a trial is the same—measured, corrective, and instructional. Like a good parent, God is always for you and never against you. His discipline can be life-changing, and, in the end, God's goal is to make you more like his Son, Jesus Christ.

James 1:12 promises, "Blessed is the man who perseveres under trial."

Hebrews 12:11: "No discipline seems pleasant at the time, but painful. Later on, however, it produces a harvest of righteousness and peace for those who have been trained by it."

At some point in your life you have probably paid for vocational training (e.g., tuition for a college or a trade school course). You paid the price and received the training. God-based, spiritual training is similar, but the price you pay is the painful experience of the trial.

On-the-job trials are like training sessions: you pay a price, they have a beginning and an end, and you are a better person for having completed the course the right way. Don't waste your next trial by merely coping or complaining. Instead, learn something meaningful and become stronger as a result of the experience.

God promises that the fruit of your trial-based learning will be a "harvest of righteousness and peace."

🌿 Magnify God and not your trials.

24

FIND STRENGTH IN THE LORD

First Samuel 30 speaks to the issue of finding strength in the Lord when others reject you.

The chapter opens with the Amalekites raiding Ziklag, a city in Judah, while David and his men were away. The powerful Amalekites carried off Judah's defenseless families, every woman and child, and burned the city.

David encouraged himself.

Upon discovering their loss, all of David's men turned against him. Suddenly, while facing this extreme trial, David found himself alone, isolated, and with no one to turn to.

David's response to his situation is recorded in 1 Samuel 30:6: "But David found strength in the Lord his God." The KJV translation says, "But David encouraged himself in the Lord his God."

David's handling of his peers' rejection contains a life lesson for every believer. When rejected by the others, David pressed into God and "found strength in the Lord" and "encouraged himself." He needed help, needed it quickly, and God was his only answer.

Note that every man in Judah was experiencing the same trial (i.e., families carried off and the city burned), but David is the only one who reached for God. He "encouraged himself" by proactively seeking God and this is the key.

God is enough.

God blessed David while the others rejected him. David grew strong while his men fed on each other's despair. Later in Psalm 118:8, David would write, "It is better to take refuge in the Lord than to trust in man."

Hebrews 11:6 promises that God "rewards those who earnestly seek him."

How did the story end?

David ultimately convinced some of the men to follow his lead, and together they pursued the Amalekites. God strengthened David who, in turn, strengthened those around him.

First Samuel 30:18–19 tells us what happened: "David recovered everything the Amalekites had taken, including his two wives. Nothing was missing: young or old, boy or girl, plunder or anything else they had taken. David brought everything back."

After finding "strength in the Lord," David led his people to victory, and this is what God wants you to remember. God will strengthen and encourage you when you turn to him in faith. God is all you need. God is enough.

Romans 8:31 asks this question of every Christian: "If God is for us, who can be against us?"

When speaking to the early church in Acts 9:31, Paul declares, "I was strengthened; and encouraged by the Holy Spirit."

🌿 "May our Lord Jesus Christ himself and God our Father... encourage your hearts and strengthen you in every good deed and word." (2 Thess. 2:16–17)

SUMMARY OF PART TWO

Workplace Trials

Key Principles

13. Toil, Thorns, and Sweat: The post-Eden, work-related effects of original sin are still active today. Your on-the-job trials are the contemporary manifestations of the "painful toil...thorns and thistles...and sweat" declared in Genesis 3. Sin is why jobs are stressful, why organizations falter, and why people experience conflict.

14. God and Your Career Trials: Trials are inevitable; they are the consequence of living and working in our fallen world. God promises you, the Christian, that he can bring good out of all things, and this includes all of your workplace challenges.

15. Two Facts about Your Trials: Your obedience to God may result in an immediate trial with the world. But, in the end, God will be there when you turn and call to him. In times of trial, maintain your resolve, and don't second guess your faithfulness.

16. Joseph: From Slave to Ruler: Trust God when others betray you. Remain upright and faithful despite your unfair treatment by others. God's plans for you are bigger than any trial you will ever face.

17. How to Build Character: Character transcends education, training, and position. It is built rather than bestowed. The development of your character requires persevering through your battles. Perseverance is engagement with the expectation of victory.

18. Four Keys to Effective Prayer: Get right with God, pray his will, keep praying, and believe for his answer. God will always do what is best for you.

19. Today's Goliaths: There are some in the workplace who will bring a fight to you. You and your Lord Jesus Christ are the targets. Don't stoop to their low tactics. Face your Goliath God's way and expect a victory.

20. Dealing with Extreme Stress: Christians are not immune to hardship. But the way we deal with our hardship sets us apart from the rest of the world. With God's help you can handle any stressful situation that comes your way.

21. Four Reasons Why God Delays: God's delay is not his denial: his ways are higher than your ways, he wants you to demonstrate your faith while you are waiting for him, he wants to bless your waiting, and he wants to be glorified when his answer arrives.

22. The Believer's Sifting: When God sifts you through a post-salvation trial, you become like good wheat: cleaner, more valuable, and ready for use. Every Christian can trust in the intercessory power of Jesus Christ.

23. Trials as Training: On-the-job trials are like training sessions: you pay a price, they have a beginning and an end, and you are a better person for having completed the course. Magnify God and not your trials.

24. Find Strength in the Lord: When rejected by others, find strength and encouragement in the Lord. He is enough. God rewards those who seek him.

Key Verses

Genesis 3:17–19: "Cursed is the ground because of you; through painful toil you will eat of it all the days of your life. It will produce thorns and thistles for you, and you will eat the plants of the field. By the sweat of your brow you will eat your food."

Genesis 39:2–3: The Lord was with Joseph and he prospered, and he lived in the house of his Egyptian master...the Lord gave him success in everything he did.

1 Samuel 17:50: So David triumphed over the Philistine with a sling and a stone; without a sword in his hand he struck down the Philistine and killed him.

1 Samuel 30:6c: But David found strength in the Lord his God.

Psalm 105:4: Look to the Lord and his strength; seek his face always.

Proverbs 3:5: Trust in the Lord with all your heart and lean not on your own understanding.

Proverbs 21:21: He who pursues righteousness and love finds life, prosperity and honor.

Isaiah 55:8–9: For my thoughts are not your thoughts, neither are your ways my ways…As the heavens are higher than the earth, so are my ways higher than your ways and my thoughts than your thoughts.

Matthew 21:22: "If you believe, you will receive whatever you ask for in prayer."

Mark 6:45–48: Immediately Jesus made his disciples get into the boat and go on ahead of him to Bethsaida, while he dismissed the crowd. After leaving them, he went up on a mountainside to pray. When evening came, the boat was in the middle of the lake, and he was alone on land. He saw the disciples straining at the oars, because the wind was against them.

Mark 6:51: Then he climbed into the boat with them, and the wind died down. They were completely amazed.

Mark 11:24: "Therefore I tell you, whatever you ask for in prayer, believe that you have received it, and it will be yours."

Luke 22:31–32: "Simon, Simon, Satan has asked to sift you as wheat. But I have prayed for you, Simon, that your faith may not fail. And when you have turned back, strengthen your brothers."

Romans 5:3–5a: Not only so, but we also rejoice in our sufferings, because we know that suffering produces perseverance; perseverance, character; and character, hope. And hope does not disappoint us.

Romans 8:28: And we know that in all things God works for the good of those who love him, who have been called according to his purpose.

Romans 8:35 and 37: Who shall separate us from the love of Christ? Shall trouble or hardship or persecution or famine or nakedness or danger or sword?...No, in all these things we are more than conquerors through him who loved us.

2 Corinthians 1:8–9: We do not want you to be uninformed, brothers, about the hardships we suffered in the province of Asia. We were under great pressure, far beyond our ability to endure, so that we despaired even of life. Indeed, in our hearts we felt the sentence of death. But this happened that we might not rely on ourselves but on God.

Galatians 6:9: Let us not become weary in doing good, for at the proper time we will reap a harvest if we do not give up.

Hebrews 10:36: You need to persevere so that when you have done the will of God, you will receive what he has promised.

Hebrews 12:7a and 11: Endure hardship as discipline; God is treating you as sons...No discipline seems pleasant at the time, but painful. Later on, however, it produces a harvest of righteousness and peace for those who have been trained by it.

James 1:12: Blessed is the man who perseveres under trial, because when he has stood the test, he will receive the crown of life that God has promised to those who love him.

James 5:16b: The prayer of a righteous man is powerful and effective.

1 John 5:14–15: This is the confidence we have in approaching God: that if we ask anything according to his will, he hears us. And if we know that he hears us—whatever we ask—we know that we have what we asked of him.

FOCUS QUESTIONS

Genesis 3:17–19 says the ground was cursed but not human work. How is this fact demonstrated in your job today? In what ways has original sin affected your work-life?

Consider these excerpts from Genesis 3:17–19: "painful toil… It will produce thorns and thistles…By the sweat of your brow." Do any of these phrases describe your work trials today?

Read Romans 8:28. This verse says God can bring good out of all things. Describe a good thing that came about as a result of a trial you experienced.

Mark 6:51 says the disciples were amazed when Jesus climbed into their boat and delivered them from their trial on the lake. When was the last time Jesus amazed you with his intervention into your life?

Read Genesis 39:2–3. God honored Joseph's consistent faithfulness by giving him "success in everything he did." Describe a time when your faithfulness to God resulted in a successful outcome to a difficult situation.

Are you praying for something now but God has not yet provided his answer? What are some reasons why God may be delaying his response?

Read James 1:12. How is perseverance different from merely coping?

Have you ever had a current-day Goliath bring a fight to you? How did you handle it?

What are some positive ways to deal with the stress in your work-life? The negative ways?

Have you ever helped another person get through a difficult trial? What is your relationship like with that person today? Has someone helped you get through a past trial? What is your opinion of that person today?

Describe a time when you obeyed God by doing the right thing, and the world pushed back.

When do people generally press into God—in times of trial or in times of prosperity? Why?

What is the most important life lesson you learned as the result of a serious trial?

Read 1 John 5:14–15. Give examples of answered prayer in your life.

PART THREE

FRUIT AND BLESSINGS

25

ALL HARD WORK
BRINGS A PROFIT

PROVERBS 14:23 ASSERTS an important work principle when it declares, "All hard work brings a profit." In this verse God promises that "all hard work" performed under his governance will always pay off.

The profit God speaks of in this verse is what is left over when your work is complete. It's the impact of your efforts, both the near and the far-reaching; it's the gain from your labor.

Your work will always bring a reward to God, self, and others—no matter what.

For most of us, work assures a profit in the form of a regular paycheck. Paychecks are nice, and big paychecks are even nicer. Proverbs 28:19 says, "He who works his land will have abundant food."

A widespread and long-lasting profit

But God's profit is not limited to pecuniary gain. Financial reward can be part of your profit, but it isn't the whole profit, and this is what God wants you to understand. For example, teachers earn paychecks, but their students go on to lead better lives as the result of what they learned in their teacher's classroom; farmers sell their crops for a profit, but their labor feeds the nations; a construction worker is paid to build a house, but the house will be the home for a growing family. Health care workers heal, leaders inspire, and policemen protect.

God intends for the impact of your labors to be good, widespread, and long-lasting. This is what he means by profit.

The profit from your labor can be realized immediately or much later—it can even live on for years after you, the worker, are gone. Your work can be a blessing to your family, employer, coworkers, customers, neighbors, and community and to others whom you do not even know.

The profit from your honorable work will always come at some time and to somebody. Why? Because God says so. The overall fruits of your labor are never small things.

The impact of your good work is much larger than the task at hand and the paycheck at the end of the day.

Whether you are a paid employee or a volunteer doing an act of service or whether your work seems insignificant or unappreciated at the time, the profit God promises in Proverbs 14:23 is guaranteed.

🌿 Find the larger profit in your everyday work.

26

CHOOSING RIGHTEOUSNESS

ARE YOU FACING a moral dilemma in your job, or are you tempted to do something unethical? Don't compromise. Do the right thing. Choose righteousness.

Every time you have the opportunity to choose between right and wrong in the workplace consider the following five verses.

Psalm 1:6: "For the Lord watches over the way of the righteous."
Proverbs 10:3: "The Lord does not let the righteous go hungry."
Proverbs 10:6: "Blessings crown the head of the righteous."
Proverbs 11:23: "The desire of the righteous ends only in good."
Proverbs 29:2: "When the righteous thrive, the people rejoice."

Righteous people will never go hungry. They will thrive. Righteous people stand out in the world, and others rejoice in their success. God watches over those who live a righteous life. The righteous way ends only in good.

Know that doing what is sound, reputable, and honest will always win the day.

The Old Testament root of the word "righteous" expresses straightness as in the word picture of staying on the straight path. Proverbs 15:21 says, "A man of understanding keeps a straight course."

God has given you a moral compass to point you in the right direction, which will be the most fruitful direction. He has equipped you to take the straight course which is always the most certain course.

God's value system never fails. Do what is right according to God's Word, and trust the results of your decisions to his sovereignty.

Isaiah 26:7 says, "The path of the righteous is level." A level path has fewer obstacles and yields a more productive journey. It is the most reliable path to get you to your desired destination.

Sometimes doing what is right in your job will result in conflict with a coworker or customer. When this happens trust in Psalm 34:19 which promises, "A righteous man may have many troubles, but the Lord delivers him from them all."

🌿 What would your life be like today if you had always made the righteous choice?

27

INSIGHTS FROM A HIGH ACHIEVER

KING SOLOMON IS an example of a person who understood exceptional achievement. He worked hard and "became greater by far than anyone."

In Ecclesiastes 2:4–10, Solomon describes the scope of his success this way:

"I undertook great projects: I built houses for myself and planted vineyards. I made gardens and parks and planted all kinds of fruit trees in them. I made reservoirs to water groves of flourishing trees. I bought male and female slaves and had other slaves who were born in my house. I also owned more herds and flocks than anyone in Jerusalem before me. I amassed silver and gold for myself, and the treasure of kings and provinces. I acquired men and women singers, and a harem as well—the delights of the heart of man. I became greater by far than anyone in Jerusalem before me. In all this my wisdom stayed with me. I denied myself nothing my eyes desired; I refused my heart no pleasure. My heart took delight in all my work, and this was the reward for all my labor."

Solomon was a high achiever of the nth degree. Today, he could be the keynote speaker at any motivational seminar and a role model for the success-driven masses.

Surely, a man who "amassed silver and gold...and the treasure of kings" was fulfilled in his career? A man who could say "I denied myself nothing" was satisfied and at peace with his choices, right?

Well, no, not really.

Everything was meaningless.

Solomon's message doesn't stop with Ecclesiastes 2:4–10. He went on to write Ecclesiastes 2:11 where he says, "Yet when I surveyed all that my hands had done and what I had toiled to achieve, everything was meaningless, a chasing after the wind; nothing was gained under the sun."

The key phrase in Ecclesiastes 2:11 is "everything was meaningless." The Hebrew word for "meaningless" means unsatisfactory, ephemeral, or transitory. Meaningless, as in the word picture of a vapor that appears quickly and then dissipates and vanishes.

Solomon wrote Ecclesiastes 2:4–11 toward the end of his life after he realized he had focused too much on the temporal and not enough on the eternal. He had narrowed his perspective to the natural and shut out the divine—too much self and not enough Spirit, too much world and not enough God.

Solomon is not saying his career achievements (i.e., what his "hands had done"), were of no value. He is saying they were temporal and fleeting.

He built houses and planted vineyards, which are both good things for this life. But he began to ask himself, "Where is God in all of this? What am I doing to serve him today and to prepare for my life in heaven tomorrow?"

Solomon had come to understand that the worldly achievements he and others thought to be so impressive were, in fact, contributing nothing to his eternal destiny. Hence, his achievements became meaningless.

Solomon would understand James 4:14: "What is your life? You are a mist that appears for a little while and then vanishes."

🖋 "What good is it for a man to gain the whole world, and yet lose, or forfeit, his very self?" (Luke 9:25)

28

FIVE CONDITIONAL BLESSINGS

PROVERBS 3:1–12 REVEALS the five blessings that will come to pass when you place God at the center of your life. This passage speaks to the biblical principle of conditional blessings, which is, in short, you do your part, and God will do his.

The Proverbs 3:1–12 passage declares that God's blessings will come when you do the following:

Do not forget my teaching, but keep my commands… Let love and faithfulness never leave you…Trust in the Lord with all your heart and lean not on your own understanding; in all your ways acknowledge him… fear the Lord and shun evil…Honor the Lord with your wealth, with the firstfruits of all your crops.

Practice these things—obedience, love, faithfulness, trust, respect, and honor—and the following Proverbs 3:1–12 blessings (i.e., conditional blessings) will be yours.

God "will prolong your life many years and bring you prosperity." (Prov. 3:2)

"Prosperity" in this verse is the word *shalom* meaning peace, health, and tranquility. God will reward your obedience with a shalom life, which is a long and peaceful life.

Shalom is the fruit of your new life in Jesus Christ who is described in Isaiah 9:6 as "Everlasting Father, Prince of Peace."

"You will win favor and a good name in the sight of God and man."(Prov. 3:4)

Doing things God's way will improve your relationships in others. You will "win favor and a good name."

God "will make your paths straight." (Prov. 3:6)

God knows the right paths to get you to the right places at the right time. Remaining faithful to him will keep you on course to a better life.

"This will bring health to your body and nourishment to your bones." (Prov. 3:8)

The word "body" is translated from the Hebrew word meaning "navel," as in a newborn baby's umbilical cord. Honoring God with your body will improve your health and well-being. Look to God for your spiritual nourishment.

"Your barns will be filled to overflowing, and your vats will brim over with new wine." (Prov. 3:10)

Give back to God. But don't give to get—give to honor your Giver. Barns and vats are material possessions. God can fill them to the brim and make them overflow, not to your glory but to his.

Finally, what do you do if the blessings of Proverbs 3:1–10 seem to be passing you by? God's answer is revealed in Proverbs 3:11–12: "My son, do not despise the Lord's discipline and do not resent his rebuke, because the Lord disciplines those he loves, as a father the son he delights in." To be disciplined by God is to be loved by God.

You do your part, and God will do his.

29

TWO SUCCESS PRINCIPLES

PSALM 1:1–3 REVEALS two principles to guide you as you pursue success in your career.

These principles are completely trustworthy. They come from an impeccable source, God's Word, and they have been tested over the centuries and proven to be reliable. The passage reads:

> Blessed is the man who does not walk in the counsel of the wicked or stand in the way of sinners or sit in the seat of mockers. But his delight is in the law of the Lord, and on his law he meditates day and night. He is like a tree planted by streams of water, which yields its fruit in season and whose leaf does not wither. Whatever he does prospers.

These verses are telling you to do the following:

Avoid ungodly influences.

Psalm 1 begins by warning you to not "walk…stand…or sit" with "the wicked…sinners…[or] mockers." The people you spend your time with will influence your destiny.

"Man" used here means human being, or person, and refers to both male and female.

You can't always choose your coworkers, but you can choose who you seek out and befriend in the workplace. Associate with productive and positive people. Choose friends of good character—avoid the unscrupulous and the ungodly.

First Corinthians 15:33 is speaking to believers when it says, "Do not be misled: 'Bad company corrupts good character,'" and Proverbs 12:26, "A righteous man is cautious in friendship."

Be a Christian witness to all, but be selective when choosing your close associates and organizational affiliations.

Stay close to God's Word.

The surest way to be successful in life is to stay close to God's Word—speak it internally in your heart and use it as a guide for your everyday choices. "Delight in the law of the Lord" and meditate on it day and night.

Culture-driven definitions of what is good, right, and valuable come and go, but Isaiah 40:8 declares, "The grass withers and the flowers fall, but the word of our God stands forever."

We will all be tempted with unethical shortcuts and worldly compromises, but doings things God's way will always bring the best results. Obedience to God is never a mistake.

Finally, the reward for the person who avoids ungodly influences and stays close to God's Word is revealed at the end of the passage in Psalm 1:3: "Whatever he does prospers." To prosper used here means to advance, to move forward, and to become successful.

🌿 "'For I know the plans I have for you,' declares the Lord, 'plans to prosper you and not to harm you, plans to give you hope and a future.'" (Jer. 29:11)

30

RUTH: A BLESSED LABORER

R UTH WAS A great woman. She is recorded by name
in the genealogy of Christ in the gospel of Matthew,
and she also has her own book in the Old Testament.

Chapters two and three of the book of Ruth describe her activities as an agricultural worker. In the world's eyes Ruth was just another unskilled laborer, but God saw her as a faithful believer whose legacy would be a blessing to mankind.

Ruth grew up in the culture of Moab and knew nothing of the God of Israel. When she became of age, Ruth joined an Israelite family by marriage.

Later, while still living in Moab, both Ruth and her Israelite mother-in-law, Naomi, became widows. With no support or prospects for a stable future, Naomi decided to leave Moab and return to her home in Bethlehem in Judah. Naomi told Ruth to stay in Moab with her birth family, but Ruth refused.

Ruth 1:16 records Ruth's words to Naomi: "But Ruth replied, 'Don't urge me to leave you or to turn back from you.

Where you go I will go, and where you stay I will stay. Your people will be my people and your God my God.'"

This verse is Ruth's statement of faith in the God of Israel. With these words Ruth placed her future in God's hands. She accompanied Naomi to Bethlehem and arrived there as a hopeful but destitute widow.

Ruth: A Common Laborer

Ruth immediately did the only work she could, which was to glean the leftover grain from a landowner's field. In the language of today's workplace, we could say Ruth took the first minimum wage job she could find.

Ruth 2:2–3 records it this way: "And Ruth the Moabites said to Naomi, 'Let me go to the fields and pick up the leftover grain behind anyone in whose eyes I find favor.' Naomi said to her, 'Go ahead, my daughter.' So she went out and began to glean in the fields behind the harvesters."

Ruth trusted God, worked, and took care of her mother-in-law. Meanwhile—and this is the point of the story—God was working behind the scenes in Ruth's life.

Ruth: A Blessed Laborer

Ruth didn't know it, but the field she chose to glean was owned by a man named Boaz.

Boaz tells her in Ruth 2:12, "May the Lord repay you for what you have done. May you be richly rewarded by the Lord, the God of Israel, under whose wings you have come to take refuge."

Scholars tell us that Boaz, a wealthy and honorable landowner, was an Old Testament foreshadow of Jesus Christ. Boaz was Ruth's redeemer just as Jesus Christ is your redeemer. God blessed Ruth's faithfulness through the person of Boaz, and he will bless your faithfulness through the Person of Jesus Christ. Boaz protected Ruth and cared for her just as Jesus does for you.

In the end Boaz and Ruth married and became the great-grandparents of King David and the direct ancestors of David's Messiah, Jesus Christ.

God worked his sovereign will for Ruth in the midst of her everyday work experiences, and he can do the same for you and every believer. He is a providential God who continually provides for his people.

Hebrews 11:6 had not been written at the time of Ruth, but its eternal truth was active in her life just as it is in yours today: "And without faith it is impossible to please God, because anyone who comes to him must believe that he exists and that he rewards those who earnestly seek him."

Remain faithful despite life's many challenges.

🌿 God is at work behind the scenes in your life.

31

BOAZ: GOD'S AGENT
OF BLESSING

Boaz's life demonstrates how God can use a working believer to be his agent of blessing to another person. Boaz's story is recorded in the book of Ruth where God uses Boaz, a wealthy landowner, to be a blessing to Ruth, a widowed laborer.

This spiritual principle of being God's agent of blessing to another person is still active today. Consider Boaz's example in the following verses from Ruth 2.

Ruth 2:2 introduces Boaz with these words: "Now Naomi had a relative on her husband's side, from the clan of Elimelech, a man of standing, whose name was Boaz."

Boaz was a "man of standing," which in Hebrew means a man of influence, substance, riches, and valor. The KJV describes Boaz as "a mighty man of wealth." In today's culture we could describe him as a mature and wealthy believer with a successful career.

In an act of divine providence, God brought Ruth to Boaz's field when she was looking for work. Ruth was a righteous woman, but at this point in her life she was poor, widowed, and a new immigrant to Israel.

Ruth 2:8–9 tell us, "So Boaz said to Ruth, 'My daughter, listen to me. Don't go and glean in another field and don't go away from here…I have told the men not to touch you. And whenever you are thirsty, go and get a drink from the water jars the men have filled.'"

Boaz welcomed Ruth and encouraged her to glean the grain left behind by his harvesters. Gleaning was God's way of providing for "the poor and the alien" (Lev. 19:10) through their own honest labor.

Boaz not only encouraged Ruth to glean his field, but he was a model of virtue and generosity throughout the whole work arrangement.

Later, in Ruth 2:12, Boaz says to Ruth, "May the Lord repay you for what you have done. May you be richly rewarded by the Lord, the God of Israel, under whose wings you have come to take refuge."

Boaz understood that he was blessed by God so he could be a blessing to Ruth. He was the human agent through whom Ruth would be "richly rewarded by the Lord."

Boaz was generous with his wealth. He was obedient to God and honorable in his relationships with others. He is an exemplary role model for today's workplace Christian.

🌿 Use your success to bless others.

32

WHO ARE YOU BECOMING?

"**W**HO ARE YOU becoming?" is a far-reaching question. Your answer addresses the whole of life. It goes beyond education, title, and career. Achievement and being the best you can be are valid issues for every worker, but the person you become along the way is much more important.

We Christians are fortunate. We have the perfect role model in Jesus Christ. Our goal is to become more like him.

Jesus lived in community with others, learned a skill, and worked just like us. But what makes Jesus different is that he is the ideal human being, and there is no better person to become like than him.

The fruit of the Spirit

Who are you becoming? Galatians 5:22–23 lists the nine qualities of the "fruit of the Spirit." With Jesus's help you can personify these qualities in your life just like he did in his.

Galatians 5:22–23 declares, "But the fruit of the Spirit is love, joy, peace, patience, kindness, goodness, faithfulness, gentleness and self-control."

Note that it is the "fruit of the Spirit" and not the fruit of you. You cannot grow God's fruit—only he can. Your responsibility is to give God a place where his fruit can flourish and grow to maturity, and that place is inside—deep and personal.

God plants his spiritual seeds in you at salvation and then grows his fruit. You nurture, protect, and harvest what God has placed within you. You become the person God wants you to be, and God gets the glory. This is how Christianity works.

The "fruit of the Spirit" is like natural fruit; it is desirable and attractive. It takes time to grow, is highly visible, and is different from its surroundings. All of which describes you as you become more like Jesus Christ.

Who are you becoming? Make it your personal goal to manifest these nine qualities from Galatians 5:22–23:

Love: A willed action to seek what is good for others
Joy: Optimism independent of your circumstances
Peace: Living in harmony with God, self, and others
Patience: Endurance with the expectation of victory
Kindness: Integrity in dealing with the weak and others
Goodness: Doing the right things for the right reasons
Faithfulness: Demonstrating that you can be trusted
Gentleness: Power under control, managed strength
Self-control: Disciplined in your actions, addiction-free

Proverbs 8:19 says, "My fruit is better than fine gold; what I yield surpasses choice silver."

🍃 Become the person God wants you to be, and then give him the glory.

33

JEHOSHAPHAT'S PRAISE

WHEN FACING AN impending crisis at work, most of us do not think to pause and praise God. To many in the workplace, the thought of praising God during a crisis seems nonsensical.

But much of what seems strange to the world actually makes sense to God.

To praise God after he performs a miracle is one thing, but to praise God in anticipation of his miracle is different. This principle, praising God in anticipation of his intervention, is the core message of Jehoshaphat's story recorded in 2 Chronicles 20:1–22.

The Bible describes Jehoshaphat as a highly respected leader. He became King of Judah when only thirty-five years old. He was honorable and blessed—a man of influence and accomplishment.

Late in his reign, Jehoshaphat faced his greatest challenge when a large enemy army gathered to attack the nation of Judah. The way Jehoshaphat responded to this challenge demonstrates the power of praising God in times of crisis.

Consider the following excerpts from 2 Chronicles 20:1–22.

Second Chronicles 20:2–3 describes the prelude to the enemy attack:

"Some men came and told Jehoshaphat, 'A vast army is coming against you.'…Alarmed, Jehoshaphat resolved to inquire of the Lord."

The advance of this "vast army" was a serious threat and a matter of life or death for the people of Judah. As Judah's leader, Jehoshaphat turned to God before making any tactical decisions.

Second Chronicles 20:6 and 20:12 reveal that Jehoshaphat's first words to God were words of praise, not panic:

"O Lord, God of our fathers, are you not the God who is in heaven? You rule over all the kingdoms of the nations. Power and might are in your hand, and no one can withstand you…For we have no power to face this vast army that is attacking us. We do not know what to do, but our eyes are upon you."

Second Chronicles 20:17 provides God's response to Jehoshaphat:

"Take up your positions; stand firm and see the deliverance the Lord will give you."

Standing firm and facing the enemy demonstrated Jehoshaphat's faith. Jehoshaphat was brave, not cowardly; he was decisive, not hesitant. Jehoshaphat took God's side in the battle.

Second Chronicles 20:18–21 is the key to the story:

In these verses Jehoshaphat praises God again, but this time with "all the people of Judah and Jerusalem."

"Jehoshaphat bowed with his face to the ground, and all the people of Judah and Jerusalem fell down in worship before the Lord…and praised the Lord, the God of Israel, with very loud voice…Have faith in the Lord your God and you will be upheld…Jehoshaphat appointed men to sing to the Lord and to praise him for the splendor of his holiness as they went out at the head of the army, saying: 'Give thanks to the Lord, for his love endures forever.'"

Jehoshaphat and the people didn't cower before their enemy or blame God for their enemy's advance. Instead, they "praised the Lord" for the victory that was sure to come.

Second Chronicles 20:22 describes Jehoshaphat's God-supplied victory.

"As they began to sing and praise, the Lord set ambushes against the men of Ammon and Moab and Mount Seir who were invading Judah, and they were defeated."

The people sang praises, God set the ambushes, and together their mutual enemy was defeated. This is how God works. When facing a serious trial, be quick to praise him for his greatness before asking for his intercession.

🌿 "I call to the Lord, who is worthy of praise, and I am saved from my enemies." (Ps. 18:3)

34

INSTRUCTIONS FOR THE RICH

THERE IS NOTHING wrong with being a rich and successful Christian.

Proverbs 14:23 promises, "All hard work brings a profit," and Proverbs 10:4 says, "Diligent hands bring wealth." The diligent, hard-working Christian can expect to be blessed with profit and wealth.

Words of caution

However, God's gifts of profit and wealth come with words of caution as stated in the following passages:

- Paul says in 1 Timothy 6:10, "For the love of money is a root of all kinds of evil."
- King Solomon warns us in Ecclesiastes 5:10, "Whoever loves money never has money enough; whoever loves wealth is never satisfied."
- Jesus says in Matthew 19:23, "I tell you the truth, it is hard for a rich man to enter the kingdom of heaven."

If all this is true, and it is, how do successful Christians enjoy the fruits of their labor (i.e., money and wealth) while guarding against the pitfalls?

The answer is found in 1 Timothy 6:17–18:

> Command those who are rich in this present world not to be arrogant nor to put their hope in wealth, which is so uncertain, but to put their hope in God, who richly provides us with everything for our enjoyment. Command them to do good, to be rich in good deeds, and to be generous and willing to share.

These verses are divine instructions for "those who are rich in this present world." When your season of material abundance arrives, if it hasn't already, the 1 Timothy 6:17–18 passage is telling you to do the following three things:

Resist the temptation to become arrogant. Don't get puffed up or expect special privileges or think of yourself as better than others.

Don't put your "hope in wealth, which is so uncertain." A good job or business and its steady earnings can be here today and gone tomorrow.

Be "generous and willing to share." Your wealth starts with God who is infinitely rich. He shares his riches with you, and then instructs you to share those same riches with others.

Finally, following the instructions in 1 Timothy 6:17–18 will yield the heavenly riches promised in 1 Timothy 6:19: "In this way they will lay up treasure for themselves as a firm foundation for the coming age, so that they may take hold of the life that is truly life."

Your heavenly treasure tomorrow will exceed all of your earthly treasures today. Eternal life is truly life. It is abundant, real, and waiting.

🌿 Begin today to lay up treasures in heaven.

35

THE SECRET OF BEING CONTENT

D O YOU KNOW "the secret of being content?" Paul
did, and his days were good days despite the hard
work and challenges.

Paul is speaking to the Christian community when he refers
to this secret in Philippians 4:11–12:

> I have learned to be content whatever the circum-
> stances. I know what it is to be in need, and I know
> what it is to have plenty. I have learned the secret of
> being content in any and every situation, whether well
> fed or hungry, whether living in plenty or in want.

To be "content in any and every situation" is to be at peace
in every situation. As he matured in his faith, Paul came to
understand that with God's help he could be completely satisfied "whether well fed or hungry, whether living in plenty or in
want."

Paul knew that Jesus reigned "whatever the circumstances." Like Paul you can experience the same contentment independent of your external circumstances.

Learn to be content.

Note that Paul learned to be content. It took time and didn't happen quickly. Paul's learning was rooted in the challenges of real life, not in a training seminar or between the covers of a book.

Paul's life of faith led the way to his learning the secret. In fact Paul was in chains in a Roman prison when he wrote the book of Philippians.

The secret is him.

In the next verse, Philippians 4:13, Paul declares, "I can do everything through him who gives me strength."

The "secret of being content" is not a program or a philosophy, and it has nothing to do with your material possessions.

The secret is him.

Philippians 4:13 says, "I can...through him." The "I" and the "him" are linked together, and this is the key: the Person of Jesus Christ was Paul's "secret of being content."

The secret is to trust every circumstance to Jesus—to know his ways and to have confidence in his grace. Circumstances change, but God doesn't. Jesus will always take care of his family. Keep him at the center of your life "whether living in plenty or in want."

In the Sermon on the Mount in Matthew 6:26, Jesus says, "Look at the birds of the air; they do not sow or reap or store away in barns, and yet your heavenly Father feeds them. Are you not much more valuable than they?"

Years later Paul added in Romans 8:31, "If God is for us, who can be against us?"

🌿 With Jesus's help you can learn to be content in every season of life.

36

MOSES'S GREAT DECISION

OSES WAS BORN a Hebrew, but grew up in the house of Pharaoh where he was surrounded by status and privilege. Acts 7:22 tells us, "Moses was educated in all the wisdom of the Egyptians and was powerful in speech and action."

At the age of forty, while still part of Pharaoh's royal family, Moses made a decision that changed the course of his life. Hebrews 11:24–26 records it this way:

By faith Moses, when he had grown up, refused to be known as the son of Pharaoh's daughter. He chose to be mistreated along with the people of God rather than to enjoy the pleasures of sin for a short time. He regarded disgrace for the sake of Christ as of greater value than the treasures of Egypt, because he was looking ahead to his reward.

Moses's great decision was that he "refused to be known as the son of Pharaoh's daughter" and chose to follow the God of Israel. Moses declared his values, changed his life, and went on to change the lives of countless others.

Consider the following three aspects from his story:

Moses made his decision by faith and when he had grown up.

His decision required maturity, integrity, and trust in God. A spiritually weak person would not have done what Moses did. At this point in his life, Moses was a grown-up. He was strong and unshakable concerning the things of God.

Moses was not distracted by the world's pleasures and treasures.

He did not sell out to Pharaoh.

In the world's eyes, Moses had it made—he was a royal in the house of Pharaoh—yet he walked away. Why? Moses walked away because "He regarded disgrace for the sake of Christ [i.e., Israel's Messiah to come] as of greater value than the treasures of Egypt."

Moses chose the treasure of greater value.

Moses knew he would be mistreated by his former colleagues who would consider his actions to be a disgrace.

Moses chose to follow God despite his awareness of the personal sacrifice it would bring. Sometimes, when we choose Jesus Christ and do the right thing, the world responds with its wrath. Know that this is nothing new.

Moses's life is a living testimony to 1 Peter 4:13–14 which declares, "But rejoice that you participate in the sufferings of Christ, so that you may be overjoyed when his glory is revealed. If you are insulted because of the name of Christ, you are blessed, for the Spirit of glory and of God rests on you."

Did Moses's great decision bear good fruit?

Yes, of course it did. After leaving Pharaoh's house, Moses went on to become Israel's national hero, lawgiver, and mediator with God. He became a man of unprecedented accomplishment and worldwide influence.

Today, about thirty-five hundred years after his great decision, Moses is remembered as one of mankind's most respected leaders.

🌿 Don't sell out to the world.

37

PROTECT YOURSELF

DEUTERONOMY 6 RECORDS Moses's instructions to Israel on how to protect itself during its forthcoming prosperity in the Promised Land. After years in the wilderness, Israel was entering into the "land flowing with milk and honey." The fulfillment of God's promise of a better life was imminent, and in Deuteronomy 6:10–14 Moses instructs Israel with these words:

> "When the Lord your God brings you into the land he swore to your fathers, to Abraham, Isaac and Jacob, to give you a land with large, flourishing cities you did not build, houses filled with all kinds of good things you did not provide, wells you did not dig, and vineyards and olive groves you did not plant—then when you eat and are satisfied, *be careful that you do not forget the Lord*, who brought you out of Egypt, out of the land of slavery. *Fear the Lord your God, serve him only* and take your oaths

in his name. *Do not follow other gods, the gods of the peoples around you."* (emphasis added)

This passage reveals three principles for protecting yourself when experiencing a season of prosperity.

"Be careful that you do not forget the Lord."

God is warning you to be careful when all of life tends to be going your way.

Like Israel we tend to press into God when we have a need and then pull back when the need is satisfied. When prosperity arrives our search for God can fade. This is our human nature.

When things are going well in your career and you are thriving in your personal Promised Land "be careful that you do not forget the Lord."

Keep God in the forefront in your seasons of prosperity just as you do in your seasons of trial.

"Fear the Lord your God, serve him only."

Fear of the Lord is a reverential fear. It has nothing to do with being scared of God. It means to hold God in awe as in the expression, "My God is an awesome God."

Honor God with your success and "serve him only." Understand that your personal success is not a measure of your Christlikeness. Being rich and successful is no more a badge of holiness than being poor is a badge of virtue.

Your goal is to be like Jesus regardless of your wealth, worldly influence, or circumstance.

"Do not follow other gods, the gods of the peoples around you."

Sin is stealthy. Expect your prosperity to be a source of temptation. Guard yourself against today's idols. For example, when faith in your expertise or knowledge begins to trump faith in God, or your employer supplants God as the source of your security.

Do not let pride replace humility, or self replace Christ.

God reigns over the whole of your life whether you have a lot or just a little.

🌿 Remain Christ-centric in your prosperity.

38

THE BLESSED LIFE

I N MATTHEW 5:1–10 Jesus reveals eight personal traits that assure believers of a blessed and happy life. We call these traits the Beatitudes. The word "beatitude" comes from the Latin word *beatitido* meaning "complete happiness."

Jesus's message in Matthew 5:1–10 is counterintuitive to the world. His words were revolutionary then, and they are still revolutionary today.

The passage opens with verses 5:1–2: "Now when he saw the crowds, he went up on a mountainside and sat down. His disciples came to him, and he began to teach them, saying…"

The "he" is Jesus Christ and the "disciples" are his followers. Accept and act upon the following teachings of Jesus. Manifest all eight personal traits, and you will enjoy a blessed and happy life.

Blessed are the poor in spirit. Your human spirit works best when it yields to God's Divine Spirit. To be "poor in spirit" is to depend to God.

Exalt God and not yourself. Be obedient to John 3:30 which says, "He must become greater; I must become less."

Blessed are those who mourn. Salvation in Jesus Christ brings a new and vivid awareness of sin. Understand sin's destructive nature and mourn its influence.

Sin destroys, but Jesus Christ restores.

Blessed are the meek. Meekness has nothing to do with weakness. Biblical meekness is strength under control. The meek are blessed because they use their strength constructively.

Jesus uses the same word for "meek" in Matthew 11:29 when describing himself as "gentle and humble in heart." The meek do well in life because they are first strong and then self-controlled in that strength.

Blessed are those who hunger and thirst for righteousness. Life will always be better when you do the right things for the right reasons.

Proverbs 10:6 declares, "Blessings crown the head of the righteous."

Blessed are the merciful. Be the person who forgives the repentant and helps the weak.

James 2:13 says, "Mercy triumphs over judgment!"

Blessed are the pure in heart. Blessed and happy are those whose motives are pure. Be transparent in your dealings with others. Enjoy mutually beneficial relationships and a clear conscience.

Blessed are the peacemakers. Peacemakers are in harmony with God, self, and others. Their lives are characterized by order rather than chaos.

Proverbs 14:30 promises, "A heart at peace gives life to the body." Peaceful living is healthy living.

Blessed are those who are persecuted because of righteousness. Jesus had enemies, and you will too, and many of those enemies will be in the workplace.

In John 15:20 Jesus says, "If they persecuted me, they will persecute you." Persecution is not defeat.

🌿 Do what Jesus says and expect to be blessed.

39

THE KEYS TO GOD'S BLESSINGS

P SALM 128:1−2 GIVES you the keys to experiencing God's blessings in your life. The passage declares, "Blessed are all who fear the Lord, who walk in his ways. You will eat the fruit of your labor; blessings and prosperity will be yours."

God promises to dispense his blessings—and these are the keys—to those who "fear the Lord" and "walk in his ways."

To "fear the Lord" is to reverence him. God is worthy of your highest respect. He wants to be first place in your life and second to no one. To "walk in his ways" is to obey his Word. God does not want you to get hurt in this fallen world, and that's why he gives you his Word as a guide.

The blessings of God will follow your obedience to God which follows your respect for God. It's that simple. Respecting

God is an internal decision, and obeying him is its external demonstration.

When you "fear the Lord" and "walk in his ways," you will be blessed. Your life will have fewer mistakes, more joy, and less pain.

King Solomon affirms this in Ecclesiastes 8:12 when he says, "I know that it will go better with God-fearing men, who are reverent before God," and Isaiah declares in Isaiah 3:10, "Tell the righteous it will be well with them, for they will enjoy the fruit of their deeds."

Your respect for God and obedience to him guarantee that "You will eat the fruit of your labor; blessings and prosperity will be yours." The NKJV renders this as "When you eat the labor of your hands, you shall be happy, and it shall be well with you."

All of us are the products of our limited experiences, and we know little of what lies in our earth-bound futures. We don't know what awaits over the next hill, much less what the world, the economy, or our employers will throw at us tomorrow.

Put God in charge of your life by respecting his person and obeying his Word, and then "blessings and prosperity will be yours."

🌿 "Tell the righteous it will be well with them, for they will enjoy the fruit of their deeds." (Isa. 3:10)

40

SOLOMON'S SUCCESS STORY

I N   M A N Y   W A Y S Solomon was the most successful man in all of history. He is remembered for his exceptional wealth, influence, and intellect. He was blessed but imperfect; his life was a dichotomy of good and bad choices. Solomon loved God yet at times rebelled against him.

Human nature has not changed, and the lessons learned from Solomon's life can be applied to your life today.

How successful was Solomon?

These references from 1 Kings 1–11 tell us:

- Solomon was anointed King of Israel (1:39).
- God appeared to Solomon two times (3:5, 9:2).
- "So God said to him…'I will give you a wise and discerning heart, so that there will never have been anyone like you, nor will there ever be'" (3:11–13).

- Solomon authored 3,000 proverbs and composed 1,005 songs (4:32); he was a botanist and biologist (4:33), and owned 1,400 chariots and 12,000 horses (10:26).
- He received 666 talents of gold yearly (10:14). That's about 730,000 ounces of gold per year.
- Solomon built the magnificent Lord's Temple in Jerusalem, which housed the Ark of the Covenant (5:5, 8:1). The construction of this temple was Solomon's greatest career accomplishment.
- "King Solomon was greater in riches and wisdom than all the other kings of the earth" (10:23).
- He wrote three books of the Bible: Song of Songs, Proverbs, and Ecclesiastes.

In the midst of Solomon's great success, God commanded him not to marry women from other nations and not to follow other gods. God did this for Solomon's own good. God was protecting Solomon from himself, but Solomon did these things anyway.

First Kings 11:3 says Solomon took "seven hundred wives of royal birth and three hundred concubines, and his wives led him astray." Incredibly, the same man who built the Lord's Temple, the holiest place on earth at the time, also built altars to the pagan gods of his foreign wives.

Sin crept into Solomon's life, and it is poised to do the same to all of us.

Fear God and keep his commandments.

But Solomon's story does not end here. At the end of his reign, Solomon wrote the book of Ecclesiastes in which he declared what he ultimately learned about success, sin, and the challenges of life.

In the last chapter of Ecclesiastes, Solomon summarizes his message to those who would follow him. His words of wisdom are recorded in Ecclesiastes 12:13: "Now all has been heard; here is the conclusion of the matter: Fear God and keep his commandments, for this is the whole duty of man."

Solomon came to know that God gave us his commandments to keep us from getting hurt in a fallen world. God's commandments are here to protect us. To "fear God" means to respect and to obey him.

Solomon kept his final message simple: "Fear God and keep his commandments." Above all else this is what the most successful man in the world wants us to remember.

🌿 Career advice from the world's most successful person: "Fear the Lord and keep his commandments."

SUMMARY OF PART THREE

Fruit and Blessings

Key Principles

25. All Hard Work Brings a Profit: All work performed under God's governance will pay off. God's type of profit is not limited to just pecuniary gain. He intends for the impact of your labors to be good, widespread, and long-lasting.

26. Choosing Righteousness: When facing a moral dilemma in your job—don't compromise. Do the right thing. Choose righteousness. God's value system never fails. Doing what is sound, reputable, and honest will always win the day.

27. Insights from a High Achiever: Solomon realized late in his life that he had focused too much on the temporal and not enough on the eternal. He had narrowed his perspective to the natural and shut out the divine. Hence everything he accomplished became "meaningless" to him.

28. Five Conditional Blessings: Place God first in your life, and his blessings are sure to follow. You do your part, and God will do his. He keeps his promises, and his timing is perfect.

29. Two Success Principles: Avoid ungodly influences and stay close to God's Word. Obedience to God is never a mistake. You can't choose your coworkers, but you can choose who you seek out and befriend in the workplace.

30. Ruth: A Blessed Laborer: Remain faithful to God despite life's challenges. He is sovereign over every circumstance you will ever experience. Know that God is at work behind the scenes in your life.

31. Boaz: God's Agent of Blessing: God can use you to be his agent of blessing to another person. Be generous with your wealth, and use your success to bless others.

32. Who Are You Becoming: Career achievement is a good thing, but the person you become along the way is much more important. Manifest the following nine qualities of the fruit of the Spirit as you move forward in your career: love, joy, peace, patience, kindness, goodness, faithfulness, gentleness, and self-control.

33. Jehoshaphat's Praise: The thought of praising God during a crisis may seem nonsensical to many in the workplace. But much of what seems strange to the world actually makes sense to God. When facing a serious trial, be quick to praise God for his greatness before asking for his intercession.

34. Instructions for the Rich: There is nothing wrong with being a rich and successful Christian. When your season of material abundance arrives do the following: resist the temptation to become arrogant, don't put your hope in wealth, and be generous and willing to share.

35. The Secret of Being Content: The secret of being content is not a program, or a philosophy, and it has nothing to do with your material possessions. The secret is "him." Jesus Christ is the secret.

36. Moses's Great Decision: Don't sell out to the pleasures and treasures of this world. It isn't worth it. Declare your Christian values before others.

37. Protect Yourself: Remain Christ-centric in your prosperity. Honor God with your career success and serve him with your prosperity. Understand that your personal success is not a measure of your Christ-likeness.

38. The Blessed Life: Do what Jesus says in the opening verses of the Sermon on the Mount in Matthew 5:1–10. Embrace his eight beatitudes, and you will experience a blessed and happy life.

39. The Keys to God's Blessings: Fear the Lord and walk in his ways and you will eat the fruit of your labor. God is worthy of your highest respect. Place him in first place in your life and second to no one.

40. Solomon's Success Story: Fear God and keep his commandments—above all else this is what the most successful man in the world wants you to remember.

Key Verses

Deuteronomy 6:14: Do not follow other gods, the gods of the peoples around you.

Ruth 2:12: May the Lord repay you for what you have done. May you be richly rewarded by the Lord, the God of Israel, under whose wings you have come to take refuge.

2 Chronicles 20:18: Jehoshaphat bowed with his face to the ground, and all the people of Judah and Jerusalem fell down in worship before the Lord.

Psalm 1:1–3: Blessed is the man who does not walk in the counsel of the wicked or stand in the way of sinners or sit in the seat of mockers. But his delight is in the law of the Lord, and on his law he meditates day and night. He is like a tree planted by streams of water, which yields its fruit in season and whose leaf does not wither. Whatever he does prospers.

Psalm 18:3: I call to the Lord, who is worthy of praise, and I am saved from my enemies.

Psalm 128:1–2: Blessed are all who fear the Lord, who walk in his ways. You will eat the fruit of your labor; blessings and prosperity will be yours.

Proverbs 3:1–2: My son, do not forget my teaching, but keep my commands in your heart, for they will prolong your life many years and bring you prosperity.

Proverbs 3:9–10: Honor the Lord with your wealth, with the firstfruits of all your crops; then your barns will be filled to overflowing, and your vats will brim over with new wine.

Proverbs 10:4: Lazy hands make a man poor, but diligent hands bring wealth.

Proverbs 10:6a: Blessings crown the head of the righteous.

Proverbs 12:26a: A righteous man is cautious in friendship.

Proverbs 14:23: All hard work brings a profit, but mere talk leads only to poverty.

Proverbs 28:19: He who works his land will have abundant food, but the one who chases fantasies will have his fill of poverty.

Proverbs 29:2a: When the righteous thrive, the people rejoice.

Ecclesiastes 2:11: Yet when I surveyed all that my hands had done and what I had toiled to achieve, everything was meaningless, a chasing after the wind; nothing was gained under the sun.

Ecclesiastes 12:13: Now all has been heard; here is the conclusion of the matter: Fear God and keep his commandments, for this is the whole [duty] of man.

Matthew 5:1–10: "Blessed are the poor in spirit…Blessed are those who mourn…Blessed are the meek…Blessed are those who hunger and thirst for righteousness…Blessed are the merciful…Blessed are the pure in heart…Blessed are the peacemakers…Blessed are those who are persecuted because of righteousness.

Romans 8:31: What, then, shall we say in response to this? If God is for us, who can be against us?

Galatians 5:22–23: But the fruit of the Spirit is love, joy, peace, patience, kindness, goodness, faithfulness, gentleness and self-control. Against such things there is no law.

Philippians 4:12–13: I know what it is to be in need, and I know what it is to have plenty. I have learned the secret of being content in any and every situation, whether well fed or hungry, whether living in plenty or in want. I can do everything through him who gives me strength.

1 Timothy 6:17–18: Command those who are rich in this present world not to be arrogant nor to put their hope in wealth, which is so uncertain, but to put their hope in God, who richly provides us with everything for our enjoyment. Command them to do good, to be rich in good deeds, and to be generous and willing to share.

Hebrews 11:6: And without faith it is impossible to please God, because anyone who comes to him must believe that he exists and that he rewards those who earnestly seek him.

Hebrews 11:24–26: By faith Moses, when he had grown up, refused to be known as the son of Pharaoh's daughter. He chose to be mistreated along with the people of God rather than to enjoy the pleasures of sin for a short time. He regarded disgrace for the sake of Christ as of greater value than the treasures of Egypt, because he was looking ahead to his reward.

FOCUS QUESTIONS

Read Proverbs 14:23. What rewards are you enjoying today that are a direct result of your hard work? How does your work impact others in a positive way (e.g., your organization, coworkers, customers, family, community, etc.)?

Read Proverbs 10:6a. Give an example of when obeying God and doing the right thing paid off in a significant way. Describe a time when God surprised you with good news regarding your job or career.

Read Proverbs 12:26a. How do you be a Christian witness to all while still being "cautious in friendship?" Have you ever been asked to do something unethical at work? How did you handle it?

Read Ruth 2:12. God is omnipotent and benevolent. Give an example of a time when God worked behind the scenes and surprised you with something big.

How have you changed since the beginning of your career? Who are your role models? Who do you wish to emulate? Are you more like Jesus today than yesterday?

Moses says in Deuteronomy 6:14, "Do not follow other gods, the gods of the peoples around you." What false gods in today's workplace are trying to lure you away from Jesus and his teachings?

Describe a trial in your life when you were certain that, with Jesus's help, everything was going to work out.

Paul tells us in 1 Timothy 6:18, "Be generous and willing to share." What are some ways you can be generous to others at your place of employment?

Read Ecclesiastes 12:13. This is what King Solomon, the most successful man in the world, wants us to remember. What does "Fear God" mean to you?

PART FOUR

RELATIONSHIPS
WITH OTHERS

41

WALK WITH THE WISE

YOU CANNOT CONTROL who your coworkers are, but you can control who you choose as your workplace friends. Select your friends wisely because your choice of friends will impact your success.

Proverbs 13:20 declares, "He who walks with the wise grows wise, but a companion of fools suffers harm." This verse is God's statement of fact: you will grow wise with the right friends, and you will suffer harm with the wrong friends.

Consider Proverbs 13:20 in its two parts.

A companion of fools suffers harm.

Fools are people who delight in not understanding. They take pleasure in pursuing the wrong things, and they scoff at living wisely.

Proverbs 1:7 says, "Fools despise wisdom and discipline," and 1 Corinthians 15:33 says, "Do not be misled: 'Bad company corrupts good character.'"

140

The Hebrew word for "companion" is used 163 times in the Old Testament and is most frequently translated in the context of a herd of sheep grazing together. Companions think alike, eat the same things (literally and figuratively), and go to the same places.

Proverbs 13:20 is telling you to not have companions who pursue the wrong things in life.

He who walks with the wise grows wise.

A wise person, on the other hand, has mastered the art of living God's way. The wise are mature and competent. They are skilled at the craft of life.

Proverbs 3:14 says, "The teaching of the wise is a fountain of life." Befriend the wise and choose them to be the ones who influence your work and guide your career.

Preferring the wise as friends does not imply that you stop evangelizing the lost. Jesus's call for you to stay in the world and be his witness to all still applies. Jesus ministered to all sorts and conditions of people, fools included, and you can too.

Jesus lived and worked in the world, yet he maintained the twelve as his closest friends.

Like Jesus you can mix it up with "tax collectors and sinners" (Matt. 9:10) while not becoming the "companion of fools." Knowing where the one stops and the other begins is key.

Finally, God's Word gives us Hebrews 10:24–25, which instructs the Christian church: "And let us consider how we may spur one another on toward love and good deeds. Let us not give up meeting together, as some are in the habit of doing, but let us encourage one another."

Forge friendships with your brothers and sisters in Christ, and "encourage one another" as fellow laborers in the workplace.

🌿 Your friends, for better or for worse, will influence your destiny. Walk with the wise.

42

RESPECT YOUR EMPLOYER

CHRISTIANS RESPECT AUTHORITY. To respect someone is to show them consideration because of their position or place in your life. For example, God's Word tells children to respect their parents, church members to respect their pastors, citizens to respect the law, and employees to respect their employers.

The three verses that follow tell you to respect the people you work for. These first-century verses refer to slaves and the work they do for their masters. "Slaves" here in the NIV is translated "servants" in the KJV. Servants, whether voluntary or involuntary, comprised a large part of the labor force at that time, and many of these servants were new Christians and members of local churches. In today's context employee and employer can be substituted for slave and master.

Evaluate the degree of respect you are showing your employer in light of the following three verses.

First Peter 2:18: "Slaves, submit yourselves to your masters with all respect, not only to those who are good and considerate, but also to those who are harsh."

As a modern day worker, you have chosen your place of employment. First Peter 2:18 is telling you to submit to and respect your manager whether that person is good and considerate, harsh, or something in between. It doesn't make any difference. When it comes to your job performance, give your managers and supervisors "all respect."

To submit to your manager is to obey your manager. However, your manager's authority is limited to ethical on-the-job matters in the workplace and during work hours only. You never have to perform any work that is illegal, immoral, or against God's Word.

You have workplace rights and never have to submit to abuse, but you do have to do your job and respect your managers—as in showing them consideration—regardless of their temperament or management style. Why? Because God says so.

First Timothy 6:1: "All who are under the yoke of slavery should consider their masters worthy of full respect, so that God's name and our teaching may not be slandered."

This verse is telling you to give "full respect" to your employer. Full respect is all, whole, and every kind of respect.

Honor all of your workplace commitments. This is your Christianity in action. Do this "so that God's name and our teaching may not be slandered."

Ephesians 6:5: "Slaves, obey your earthly masters with respect and fear, and with sincerity of heart, just as you would obey Christ."

A paraphrase of this verse could read, "Employees, obey your employers just as you would obey Christ." Understand the objectives of your employer, and then do the work you are being paid to do. Fulfill all of your job responsibilities with a "sincerity of heart."

🌿 Christian employees should be the best employees in every organization.

43

DEALING WITH A FOOL

THE BOOK OF Proverbs makes over sixty references to fools and their folly. It's a big topic. A fool is the opposite of a wise person.

Proverbs reveals the following five personal characteristics of a fool with their supporting verses.

Fools cause conflict. "A fool finds pleasure in evil conduct" (Prov. 10:23). "A fool gives full vent to his anger" (Prov. 29:11). "A fool is hotheaded and reckless" (Prov. 14:16), and "Every fool is quick to quarrel" (Prov. 20:3).

Fools talk more than they listen. "A fool finds no pleasure in understanding but delights in airing his own opinions" (Prov. 18:2), "He who answers before listening—that is his folly and his shame" (Prov. 18:13), and "The heart of fools blurts out folly" (Prov. 12:23).

Fools don't learn. "Of what use is money in the hand of a fool, since he has no desire to get wisdom?" (Prov. 17:16), "As a dog returns to its vomit, so a fool repeats his folly" (Prov. 26:11), and "The way of a fool seems right to him" (Prov. 12:15).

Fools are unreliable. "Like cutting off one's feet or drinking violence is the sending of a message by the hand of a fool" (Prov. 26:6).

Employers should think twice before hiring a fool. "Like an archer who wounds at random is he who hires a fool" (Prov. 26:10), and fools don't make good business partners—"If a wise man goes to court with a fool, the fool rages and scoffs, and there is no peace" (Prov. 29:9).

Fools self-destruct. "A chattering fool comes to ruin" (Prov. 10:8), "A man's own folly ruins his life, yet his heart rages against the Lord" (Prov. 19:3). In biblical language "ruin" used here means "thrown aside" or "cast away by others." Fools blame God for their ruin instead of themselves and their own destructive behaviors.

Finally, "The wise woman builds her house, but with her own hands the foolish one tears hers down" (Prov. 14:1). Wise people build; foolish people tear down.

How do you deal with a fool?

Maintain a constructive relationship with them, guard yourself against their folly, and tell them about Jesus Christ when they are ready to hear.

Remember 1 Timothy 2:4: God "wants all men to be saved and to come to a knowledge of the truth."

No person is beyond Jesus's reach. We are not here to condemn others, but to point them to Jesus Christ and the Good News of his work at Calvary. Were we not all fools-of-a-sort before Jesus saved us?

🌿 The workplace is your mission field, fools included.

44

ENCOURAGE ONE ANOTHER

EBREWS 3:13 IS speaking to Christians when it declares, "Encourage one another daily," and 1 Thessalonians 5:11 says, "Therefore encourage one another and build each other up."

The Greek verb translated as "encourage" is *parakaleo,* which means "to call to a person." It comes from *para* (to the side) and *kaleo* (to call). The biblical word picture of an encourager is someone who stands by your side and calls you to move forward. A true encourager doesn't push or poke you from behind; they stand with you and then walk at your side as you move forward to a better place.

God the Holy Spirit is the original encourager. John refers to the Holy Spirit as the *parakletos* in John 14:16 which is translated as "Comforter" in the NIV and "Helper" in the NASB.

As the Holy Spirit encourages you, you are called to encourage others.

Barnabas, Son of Encouragement

Consider the example of Barnabas. His birth name was Joseph, but in Acts 4:36 the apostles gave him the nickname of "Barnabas which means Son of Encouragement." Barnabas's peer group recognized his gift for encouraging others and later, in Acts 9, it is Barnabas who first supports Paul, the new convert, by introducing him to the other apostles.

Acts 9:26–27 reads, "When he [Paul] came to Jerusalem, he tried to join the disciples, but they were all afraid of him, not believing that he really was a disciple. But Barnabas *took* him and brought him to the apostles. He *told* them how Saul on his journey had seen the Lord and that the Lord had spoken to him, and how in Damascus he had preached fearlessly in the name of Jesus." (emphasis added)

Barnabas "took" and "told." His encouragement of Paul involved personal action (the "took") as well as supportive words (the "told"). Barnabas, the Son of Encouragement, was there to help Paul at the precise time Paul needed to be helped.

Just as the Holy Spirit is The Helper, you are a helper. You can inspire others with your actions and words.

Paul went on to do great things for the Lord, as did Barnabas. Acts 11:24 describes Barnabas's legacy this way: "He was a good man, full of the Holy Spirit and faith, and a great number of people were brought to the Lord."

🌿 Encourage others with your supportive words and personal actions.

45

DEBORAH'S LEADERSHIP

D EBORAH WAS A wife, judge, and national leader. What she accomplished over three thousand years ago for the nation of Israel is a helpful case study in applied leadership. Her story, found in Judges 4–5, can benefit every person of influence in today's workplace.

Deborah's public life demonstrates the following characteristics of an effective leader.

Deborah led when times were difficult.

Deborah rose to leadership at a dark time in Israel's history. Israel was in decline. It had fallen away from God and was in need of a deliverer.

Judges 4:1–3 declares, "The Israelites once again did evil in the eyes of the Lord…they cried to the Lord for help." Deborah says in Judges 5:7, "Village life in Israel ceased, ceased until I, Deborah, arose, arose a mother in Israel."

Deborah arose when Israel needed new leadership to stop its fall. She did what great leaders do and that is to grow strong and step forward when times are difficult.

Deborah spoke with authority.

Leaders are subject matter experts within their sphere of influence. They add value, bring solutions, and speak with authority.

Judges 4:4 says Deborah was "a prophetess...leading Israel at the time." The nation of Israel respected Deborah as someone who spoke with authority concerning the things of God.

While you may not be a leader of Deborah's scope, you can learn to speak with authority within your own career specialty. Establish credibility by excelling at your job and helping others do the same with theirs.

Earning the respect of your coworkers is the first step toward becoming their leader.

Deborah's followers affirmed her leadership.

Leaders are magnets, not bulldozers, and Deborah was a magnet.

Judges 4:5 says, "She held court under the Palm of Deborah...and the Israelites came to her to have their disputes decided." Deborah made good use of all the gifts and opportunities God sent her way.

There is no hint in any of the Judges passages of Deborah being a self-promoter. She magnified God and served his people. Deborah's followers were better off for having spent time with her. People are attracted to the Deborahs of the world.

Deborah didn't have to fight her way up the organizational ladder. She was summoned by God and affirmed by her followers.

Deborah led by example.

Deborah, Israel's leader, called Barak, Israel's military commander, and instructed him to attack the army of Jabin, the king of Canaan, who was oppressing Israel. Barak agreed to go and fight Jabin's army but with one condition.

Judges 4:8 declares, "Barak said to her, 'If you go with me, I will go; but if you don't go with me, I won't go.'" She replies in Judges 4:9, "'Very well,' Deborah said, 'I will go with you.'"

Deborah led by example. She was not a warrior or battle commander and could have easily said she would be of better use by remaining behind, but she did not do that. She faced reality and exposed herself to the full consequences of her decision.

Under Deborah's leadership Israel's enemy was defeated, the oppression was lifted, and Israel returned to God. Her story concludes in Judges 5:31 with these final words: "Then the land had peace forty years."

🌿 Leaders are magnets, not bulldozers.

46

THE GENEROUS WORKER

CHRISTIANS ARE A generous people. Generous people are free of smallness; they are magnanimous and not petty. The Latin root of *generous* means "of noble birth." The generous person carries a mark of distinction; they give liberally and they are special.

Jesus was supremely generous.

John 3:16–17 says that because of his love for us, Jesus gave himself in order "to save the world," and 2 Corinthians 8:9 proclaims, "He was rich, yet for your sakes he became poor, so that you through his poverty might become rich." In Acts 20:35 Paul is quoting Jesus when he says, "It is more blessed to give than to receive."

Paul is speaking to Christians in 2 Corinthians 9:11 when he says, "You will be made rich in every way so that you can be generous on every occasion." Being generous on "every occasion" includes what you do at work. When you are generous, everyone wins. You and the person you help are both blessed, your team or organization improves, and God is smiling at every step.

Generous or stingy?

In the Old Testament, Proverbs 11:25 says, "A generous man will prosper; he who refreshes others will himself be refreshed." Several chapters later Proverbs 28:22 says, "A stingy man is eager to get rich and is unaware that poverty awaits him."

A "stingy man" in the NIV is translated a "man with an evil eye" in the NKJV. The stingy person is shortsighted. They think if they give something away, there will only be less for them. They are captives of zero-sum thinking, limited by a one-winner, one-loser mentality, and they are wrong.

God's ways are different. He is not bound by naturalistic thinking. God multiplies supernaturally. He guarantees that a "generous man will prosper." Those who hoard their on-the-job gifts are missing out on some of life's most rewarding opportunities.

Being generous is part of your Christian witness to others.

There are many ways to be generous in the workplace such as speaking words of encouragement, mentoring, training, assisting a new hire, helping a coworker solve a problem, sharing your expertise with another, and going the extra mile to meet a deadline.

🌿 Share your time, skills, and resources with others.

47

THE SPIRIT OF EDIFICATION

IT'S EASY FOR us Christians to say good things about our coworkers because we are endowed with the spirit of edification. We prefer to build others up rather than tear them down—this is our nature in Jesus Christ.

Paul is referring to the spirit of edification in 2 Corinthians 10:8: "For even if I boast somewhat freely about the authority the Lord gave us for building you up rather than pulling you down, I will not be ashamed of it."

In this verse Paul is telling the church that the purpose of his influence over them is "for building you up rather than pulling you down." The NKJV translates Paul's words as "for edification and not for your destruction."

When it comes to other people, we Christians do construction and not destruction.

In Matthew 22:39 Jesus says, "Love your neighbor as yourself." Your neighbor is every person who is close by whether a believer or nonbeliever, and this includes all the people at your place of employment.

To love a coworker is to wish them well. This type of love is moral and fruit-bearing—it's a sincere expression of goodwill toward others.

Consider the following verses:

Romans 15:2: "Each of us should please his neighbor for his good, to build him up."

Galatians 6:10: "Therefore, as we have opportunity, let us do good to all people."

Ephesians 4:29: "Do not let any unwholesome talk come out of your mouths, but only what is helpful for building others up according to their needs, that it may benefit those who listen."

Note the words of edification in these verses: "for his good...build him up...let us do good to all people...benefit those who listen." Affirm what is good in your employer and coworker, and support what is right and productive. This is the spirit of Christian edification.

The office critic pushes people down, but the edifying Christian lifts them up. Edification brings out the best in others. It fosters teamwork and a higher level of personal performance.

Biblical edification is not flattery, which is self-serving praise of another. The Bible associates flattery with insincerity and deviousness. Edify but don't flatter—there is a difference between the two. Psalm 12:3 says, "May the Lord cut off all flattering lips."

Most of your coworkers are doing a good job, working hard, and planning for a bright future. When you edify them, you are recognizing their worth without regard to pay scale or position. Your edification helps them become the person God wants them to be.

Romans 14:19 says, "Let us therefore make every effort to do what leads to peace and to mutual edification."

🌿 Speak to the good in others.

48

SANCTIFIED AMBITION

T HE WORKPLACE IS full of ambitious people, and rightly so. The ambitious have a strong desire to succeed. They are results-oriented, energetic, and usually accomplish what they set out to do.

When it comes to getting the job done, ambition always beats the opposite qualities of laziness and apathy. Proverbs 10:4 affirms this when it declares, "Lazy hands make a man poor, but diligent hands bring wealth."

Ambitiously working to get the most out of your career (i.e., being eager, resourceful, and enterprising), is a good thing. But, for all of its goodness, ambition has a downside, and this is what God is warning us about in Philippians 2:3: "Do nothing out of selfish ambition or vain conceit, but in humility consider others better than yourselves."

Consider Philippians 2:3 in its two parts.

"Do nothing out of selfish ambition or vain conceit."

In the language of the New Testament, those who pursue "selfish ambition" are characterized as contentious and quick to cause strife. They abuse others in their pursuit of personal gain.

Also, "vain conceit," used here in the NIV is rendered "vainglory" in the KJV. It means empty glory. The vainglorious achiever is a relentless self-promoter—puffed up and self-absorbed—a taker who burns through people and resources as so much fodder.

We all know someone like this. We don't embrace their actions and God doesn't, either.

"In humility consider others better than yourself."

This statement seems incompatible with career success, but it really isn't. God is simply telling you to show respect and deference to others.

To work hard and excel is fine, but to look down on others in the process is not. Exercise humility while delivering an excellent work product; this is always the best course of action.

Being better at your job than someone else does not mean you are morally superior to them. Success in the workplace does not necessarily correlate with success in the whole of life.

If left unchecked an overly ambitious coworker can disrupt the synergy of your team or organization. Their "I" will supersede the corporate "We."

Philippians 2:4–5 speaks to this issue of being ambitious for the success of others when it declares, "Each of you should look not only to your own interests, but also to the interests of others. Your attitude should be the same as that of Christ Jesus."

Christ Jesus is your role model and the personification of sanctified ambition. He cares about the "interests of others" and you should too.

🌿 Be ambitious for the success of others as well as your own success.

49

CHURCH AND WORK

CTS 2:42 IS describing the first Christians when it says, "They devoted themselves to the apostles' teaching and to the fellowship, to the breaking of bread and to prayer."

These early believers worked all week just like you. Yet they gathered each Sunday and "devoted themselves" to the following spiritual disciplines.

The apostles' teaching

God's Word is the surest source of work-life wisdom, and it can benefit all workers in every occupation.

Paul says in 2 Timothy 3:16, "All Scripture is God-breathed and is useful for teaching, rebuking, correcting and training in righteousness," and Proverbs 8:10 instructs you to "Choose my instruction instead of silver." In the workplace we say knowledge is power, but knowledge of God's Word is the source code of power.

Increase your understanding of "the apostles' teaching" through your local church's various ministries.

The fellowship

Christian fellowship begins vertically with Jesus Christ and extends horizontally throughout his Body, the church. The Greek word for "fellowship" is *koinonia,* which conveys partnership, communion, and close relationship.

Jesus promises you in Matthew 18:20, "For where two or three come together in my name, there am I with them." Your Christ-centric, church-based relationships allow you the freedom to learn, to grow, and to express yourself independent of the restrictions of the workplace.

The breaking of bread

In the first century, the church gathered in the homes of believers for a common meal (the bread was hard then and literally had to be broken). They joined in fellowship, worshipped God, shared his Word, and celebrated the Lord's Supper.

This is what Paul is referring to in Acts 20:7 when he declares, "On the first day of the week we came together to break bread." These home churches were the precursors to today's larger church gatherings.

The Greek word for "church" is *ekklesia,* which means an assembly or gathering of people. The whole Christian church, local and worldwide, is *ekklesia,* which is a called out gathering of like-minded individuals.

Hebrews 10:25 commands, "Let us not give up meeting together, as some are in the habit of doing." We are called to community with other believers and that community begins with our local church. Christians are not spiritual lone rangers.

Prayer

The prayer referred to here is corporate prayer. Galatians 6:2 instructs us to "Carry each other's burdens, and in this way you will fulfill the law of Christ."

Are you anxious about something at work? Do you need God's help with your job or career? Ask your church family to pray for you just as you will be praying for them. Jesus says in Matthew 21:13, "My house will be called a house of prayer."

🌿 What you do on Sunday at church makes life better from Monday through Friday at work.

50

JEALOUSY IN THE WORKPLACE

S
TRESS, COMPETITION, AND cliques—the workplace
is a breeding ground for jealousy. All of us are susceptible
to it, and most of us will never admit to it, but it is there
just the same.

The good news is with God's help you can eliminate jealousy from your life once and for all.

Begin by seeing jealousy for the destructive emotion it really is. Paul makes the serious nature of jealousy clear in Galatians 5:20 when he includes it in this list of negative behaviors: idolatry and witchcraft; hatred, discord, jealousy, fits of rage, selfish ambition, dissensions, and factions. Earlier in 1 Corinthians 3:3, Paul writes, "You are still worldly. For since there is jealousy and quarreling among you, are you not worldly?"

Jealousy goes hand in hand with "hatred...discord...fits of rage...dissensions...quarreling." Its consequences are always negative. Jealousy is "worldly" and not of God.

The source of jealousy

God teaches us about the cause of jealousy in the three passages below. All of the people in these verses, Rachel; Joseph's brothers, who were the patriarchs; and the Jews, share something in common: their own personal insecurities fueled their jealousy of another person. Your jealousy begins in you and is fed by you. You are the source of your jealousy and not the other person.

Consider the following verses:

Genesis 30:1: When Rachel saw that she was not bearing Jacob any children, she became jealous of her sister.

Acts 7:9: Because the patriarchs were jealous of Joseph, they sold him as a slave into Egypt.

Acts 13:45: When the Jews saw the crowds, they were filled with jealousy and talked abusively against what Paul was saying.

Your jealousy transfers the control of your emotions to other people; it empowers "them" instead of "you." The key to removing jealousy from your life is to take back the control.

The next time you begin to feel jealous of a coworker, use it as a warning to turn your thoughts back to your own talents and responsibilities.

Give the other person over to God and concentrate on your own resources, strengths, and goals. Do this and you will be too invested in your own good work and potential to become jealous of others. Remember 2 Corinthians 3:17: "Now the Lord is the Spirit, and where the Spirit of the Lord is, there is freedom."

🌿 "Be transformed by the renewing of your mind." (Rom. 12:2)

51

THE GOLDEN RULE

T HERE IS PROBABLY no better principle for guiding your workplace relationships than this simple statement: Treat others as you would like to be treated.

In our culture we call this the Golden Rule. It is labeled "golden" because of its great value. Following the golden rule is considered to be noble and right in almost every situation. It is applied Christianity as well as being a universally admired life principle.

The golden rule is validated by Jesus Christ in the Sermon on the Mount in Matthew 7:12: "So in everything, do to others what you would have them do to you, for this sums up the Law and the Prophets."

A summary teaching

Jesus opens and closes this verse with references to it being a summary of other New and Old Testament teachings.

The verse begins with Jesus saying, "So in everything," "So" used here in the NIV is translated "therefore" in the KJV and

NASB. By doing this Jesus is connecting the message of this verse with his previous statements (i.e., his teachings in the Sermon on the Mount).

Then Jesus ends the verse with the words, "For this sums up the Law and the Prophets," which also marks the verse as a summary statement; but these closing words refer to various Old Testament teachings.

Jesus's teaching

Jesus's core message in Matthew 7:12 is recorded in the center of the verse: "Do to others what you would have them do to you." This is the golden rule as spoken by Jesus over two thousand years ago.

Jesus is saying that you take the initiative—you "do." The golden rule begins with you. You do what is right, and then God takes care of everything else.

Following the golden rule is God's expectation for you as his representative in the workplace.

Not a salvation teaching

Finally, the golden rule is a good Bible-based guide for your dealings with others, but following the Golden Rule is not a path to salvation. People cannot save themselves by their own good works no matter how wholesome, unselfish, or well-intentioned they may be.

The Bible is clear when it says that salvation requires repentance and receiving Jesus Christ as Savior. Ephesians 2:8–9 declares, "For it is by grace you have been saved, through faith—and this not from yourselves, it is the gift of God—not by works, so that no one can boast."

❧ Treat your coworkers as you would like to be treated.

52

WORKING TO GIVE

O NE WAY TO immediately improve the quality of your work-life is to define yourself as a giver. Begin to focus on what you are giving to those who rely on your efforts (e.g., competence to your coworkers, a strong work ethic to your employer, and premier product or service to your customers).

The principle of working to give applies to all workers in all cultures and has nothing to do with job title or earnings.

Would you rather be known as a giver or a taker?

Givers are appreciated and sought after while takers are generally avoided. Givers are synergistic. They build organizations and contribute to the success of the people around them.

Think about it: who wants to work with someone who only takes?

Giving to others is part of your Christian witness to the world. Jesus instructs us in Matthew 10:8, "Freely you have received, freely give," and Acts 20:35 declares, "Lord Jesus Himself said: 'It is more blessed to give than to receive.'" The writer of Hebrews 13:16 says, "And do not forget to do good and to share with others."

Givers understand the law of sowing and reaping which is stated in 2 Corinthians 9:6 this way: "Remember this: Whoever sows sparingly will also reap sparingly, and whoever sows generously will also reap generously."

The law of sowing and reaping works the same way for everyone, every time. It never changes or stops working. There may be a season between the sowing and the reaping, but your harvest is sure to come.

Proverbs 11:24 declares, "One man gives freely, yet gains even more; another withholds unduly, but comes to poverty."

Jesus tells us more about giving in Luke 6:38: "Give, and it will be given to you. A good measure, pressed down, shaken together and running over, will be poured into your lap. For with the measure you use, it will be measured to you."

God guarantees your giving will come back to you. For example, if you give information, support, and opportunity to your coworkers—you will receive information, support, and opportunity from your coworkers.

Our flesh says if we give something away, we will not have enough left for ourselves. But Jesus Christ says the opposite. In fact the more we give the more we will reap. It's a faith principle.

🖎 Who wants to work with someone who only takes?

53

THE LEADER WHO EMPOWERS

MATTHEW 9:35–10:1 IS a story about Jesus sending out his disciples to evangelize the world. It
begins with Jesus acting alone and ministering to
the crowds and ends with him empowering his disciples to do
the very same thing. What Jesus does in the middle verses of the
passage serves as a model for empowering others to lead.

Jesus went through all the towns and villages, teaching
in their synagogues, preaching the good news of the
kingdom and healing every disease and sickness. When
he saw the crowds, *he had compassion* on them, because
they were harassed and helpless, like sheep without a
shepherd. Then he said to his disciples, "The harvest is
plentiful but the workers are few. Ask the Lord of the
harvest, therefore, to send out workers into his harvest
field." *He called his twelve disciples to him and gave them*

authority to drive out evil spirits and to heal every disease and sickness. (emphasis added)

Woven into the story are the steps Jesus took in empowering his disciples.

"Jesus went…he saw…he had compassion."

Jesus took the initiative and "went through all the towns and villages, teaching…preaching…healing." He was an active, self-motivated, and life-changing leader. Jesus "saw the crowds." He cared about them and was moved to take action. Jesus accepted responsibility for helping those who needed him.

Seek out the problems and opportunities in your sphere of influence. Be proactive. Go to where things are happening, and spend time with your coworkers and customers.

The first step toward empowering others to lead is to be an engaged and influential leader yourself.

"He called his twelve disciples to him and gave them authority."

After going to his people, seeing their needs, and being moved to take action, Jesus turned to his disciples. He could have solved the people's problems himself, but he chose to empower his disciples to help.

Jesus was a leader who raised up other leaders, and this is the key to the passage.

Jesus called his disciples to him. He would be their equipper, not someone else. He gave his disciples the authority to act in his behalf.

Jesus did not equip everyone. He only equipped the few who were ready. He called the few and then empowered them to follow his example.

The best leaders equip others by teaching the teachable and sending them out to become leaders themselves.

If God has blessed you with the ability to lead, use your gift to empower others. Remember Ephesians 4:12 which says God gives you his gifts "for the equipping of the saints for the work of ministry, for the edifying of the body of Christ" (NKJV).

🌿 Be the leader who empowers others to lead.

54

THE OFFICE ENEMY

THE BIBLE SAYS you are to love your enemies. But how do you love a hostile coworker?

This is the person who, for whatever reason, goes beyond being merely difficult. These people engage in harmful activities that undermine your reputation or work product, and their actions are serious. How do you respond?

Jesus addresses this issue in the Sermon on the Mount in Matthew 5:38–44.

> "You have heard that it was said, 'Eye for eye, and tooth for tooth.' But I tell you, Do not resist an evil person. If someone strikes you on the right cheek, turn to him the other also. And if someone wants to sue you and take your tunic, let him have your cloak as well. If someone forces you to go one mile, go with him two miles. Give to the one who asks you, and do not turn away from the one who wants to borrow from you. You have heard

that it was said, 'Love your neighbor and hate your enemy.' But I tell you: Love your enemies and pray for those who persecute you."

How do you "love your enemies?" Follow what Jesus said:

Do not engage in eye for eye retaliation.

Jesus introduces this point by saying "You have heard" before quoting the famous "eye for eye" law from Exodus 21:23–25. God originally dictated the "eye for eye" law to Moses on Mount Sinai as civil law for the governance of Israel.

Jesus is saying that for a Christian to use the "eye for eye" law today as justification for acts of retribution toward others is to misapply his Word.

God's purpose for the "eye for eye" law was to limit personal retaliation for an offense by addressing the sinful practice of unlimited retaliation.

Under the "eye for eye" law, Exodus 21:24–25 declares that the wronged Israelite could respond with an "eye for eye, tooth for tooth, hand for hand, foot for foot, burn for burn, wound for wound, bruise for bruise," but no more. The spirit of the "eye for eye" law was to limit conflict in ancient Israel, and never to justify increased conflict.

However, and most importantly, the "eye for eye" law does not apply to today's Christian. First Peter 3:9 says, "Do not repay evil with evil or insult with insult." We Christians are not "eye for eye" people.

Do not resist like an evil person.

"Do not resist" means to not respond to an evil person with the same wicked tactics they have directed toward you.

For example, if a coworker is telling destructive lies about you, do not respond by telling destructive lies about him. Instead, speak truth to the lies and respond wisely and with integrity.

Your Christlike demeanor and professional actions will speak for themselves despite the claims of an evil coworker.

Also, the Matthew 5:38–44 passage does not say you must endure abuse from others. Both believers and unbelievers alike have the right to protect themselves. If your office enemy engages in physical assault, bullying, discrimination, sexual harassment, or any other evil action, you have recourse through your employer as well as civil law enforcement and the legal system.

Turn the other cheek.

This means to simply choose your battles. The "cheek… cloak…miles" references are metaphors for less serious offenses that do not require you to take action. You do not have to respond to every jab from a hostile coworker. Sometimes it will be best to let a minor offense go.

Love your enemies and pray for those who persecute you.

This is the key to what Jesus is saying in Matthew 5:38–44: Love your office enemy the same way he loves your office enemy.

Proverbs 25:21–22 declares, "If your enemy is hungry, give him food to eat; if he is thirsty, give him water to drink. In doing this, you will heap burning coals on his head, and the Lord will reward you."

❧ Do not be an "eye for eye" person.

THE SERVANT LEADER

L EADERS INFLUENCE OTHERS. They can be great or common, young or old. If your work influences others, you are a leader.

Jesus taught real-time, hands-on leadership by his example. He is the embodiment of personal greatness and the world's most successful servant leader. Jesus defines the qualities of a servant leader in his own words in Mark 10:42–45.

Consider this passage in its three parts.

Jesus begins in Mark 10:42 by describing the least effective way to lead others.

> Jesus called them together and said, "You know that those who are regarded as rulers of the Gentiles lord it over them, and their high officials exercise authority over them."

Jesus uses the phrase "over them" twice in this single verse and both times with negative connotations. These "rulers" and "high officials" who "lord" their authority over others are the antithesis of the servant leader. They are driven by rank, rules, and hierarchy. They control but do not inspire.

These command-and-control rulers exalt themselves at the expense of their organizations and others.

In Mark 10:43–44 Jesus describes God's type of leader, which is the servant leader.

> "Not so with you. Instead, whoever wants to become great among you must be your servant, and whoever wants to be first must be slave of all."

Note that Jesus does not rebuke his disciples for wanting "to become great." The word "great" refers to persons who are eminent for their ability or authority. "Great" has the same root as the English prefix *mega*. As a working Christian you can develop mega-abilities, exercise mega-authority, and become a mega-person of great influence. It's all okay with God so long as you honor him throughout the process.

If God has gifted you to become a great person in your chosen field, say yes to his gift, get to work, and give him the glory along the way.

Jesus says a great Christian is a servant. In today's workplace the servant leader builds the people who will build the organization. They are positive and motivating, and they bring out the best in others.

In Mark 10:45 Jesus says he came to serve.

"For even the Son of Man did not come to be served, but to serve, and to give his life as a ransom for many."

From Calvary to today, Jesus continues to change people's lives for the better. He does it not by being served but by serving others. Jesus is the perfect servant leader. Follow his example—become a servant leader too.

🌿 Bring out the best in the people you work with.

56

WOLVES AT WORK

T HERE ARE SOME in the workplace who are actively anti-Christian. They have little use for Jesus Christ and, as one of his people, little use for you.

Jesus speaks to this reality in the gospel of Matthew. When sending out his twelve disciples, Jesus says, in Matthew 10:16, "I am sending you out like sheep among wolves. Therefore be as shrewd as snakes and as innocent as doves."

This verse is both a warning about the "wolves" in your midst and an instruction on how to deal with them. Consider Matthew 10:16 in its five parts.

"I am sending you out"

Jesus sends you and every other Christian out and into the world. In John 17:18 Jesus says to his Father, "I have sent them into the world." When you go to work every day you are part of the "them." You are serving God in the workplace, which, in many ways, is Christianity's front line.

Your work is Kingdom work, and you are the King's representative at your place of employment.

"Like sheep among wolves"

Sheep and wolves have different natures. Wolves attack sheep, especially the weak, and they are ruthless. First John 3:13 confirms this reality: "Do not be surprised, my brothers, if the world hates you."

"Therefore"

Since God has purposefully sent you out into the midst of wolves, he now tells you what to do while in their company.

"Be as shrewd as snakes"

Snakes are almost universally disliked, but here in Matthew 10:16 Jesus is applying one of their redeeming attributes, which is to know when to avoid confrontation. Snakes excel at self-preservation, and Jesus is telling you to do the same. There will be times in the workplace when it is best to be shrewd and to leave the wolves to themselves.

The fact is you are not required to debate every anti-Christian wolf in every situation that comes your way. Many of these types of debates are a waste of time. Instead, Jesus is instructing us to be shrewd (i.e., skillful, intelligent, and wise), and to use discernment.

This is the same thing Jesus is saying in Matthew 7:6: "Do not give dogs what is sacred; do not throw your pearls to pigs. If you do, they may trample them under their feet, and then turn and tear you to pieces."

An unbeliever seeking truth is one thing, but a wolf who is looking for a fight is something different.

"And as innocent as doves"

To be innocent means to be unmixed with evil intent.

As one of God's doves, you are equipped to exercise self-control and integrity. Take the high road when responding to the wolves, and do not mimic their destructive behavior. Instead, respond to them on God's terms, in God's ways, and according to his timing.

Finally, the wolves won't admit it but doves are respected. People are drawn to doves, and you may be the spiritual dove God is using to reach the wolf at your workplace.

First Timothy 2:4 declares that God "wants all men to be saved and to come to a knowledge of the truth."

Maintain a productive work relationship with your anti-Christian coworkers, and when they are ready to listen, tell them how Jesus Christ changed your life for the better.

🕊 Share Jesus with those who are ready to hear.

57

GLORIFYING GOD AT WORK

THE ULTIMATE PURPOSE of life is to glorify God. This is why you were born.

In 1 Corinthians 10:31 Paul affirms the supreme importance of this when he declares, "Whatever you do, do it all for the glory of God." The "whatever you do" includes all of your activities and relationships.

For example, God calls you to glorify him in your home and community, with your friends as well as strangers, in marriage or singleness, and very definitely in your daily work in which you "do it all for the glory of God."

God's glory can be defined as the manifestation of his presence. His glory is not an abstract concept; it can be seen and sensed in the world, and it can be experienced.

Isaiah 6:3 tells us, "The whole earth is full of his glory."

As Christians we are alive with Christ, and by his grace we have the greatest capacity, more than any other created thing, to glorify him in the way we live.

Jesus has already given us the Father's glory.

He says so in John 17:22: "I have given them the glory that you gave me." We Christians do not have to go find God's glory—it was God's gift to us at the time of our salvation.

God has planted his glory in every Christian, and he desires for us to radiate it before others. This is what Jesus is saying to his followers in Galilee in Matthew 5:16:

> "In the same way, let your light shine before men, that they may see your good deeds and praise your Father in heaven."

Today, your light (i.e., Christian character, work ethic, demeanor, and "good deeds" in the workplace), reflect positively on your "Father in heaven" and bring glory to him. God always gets the glory, never us.

Jesus says in Matthew 5:15, "Neither do people light a lamp and put it under a bowl. Instead they put it on its stand, and it gives light to everyone in the house."

Glorifying God at work is like the shining lamp on a stand. Talking about light is one thing, but being the lamp that illuminates your surroundings is all together more real and meaningful.

Ask yourself these on-the-job questions:

- Are my actions bringing glory to God?
- Do my words align with God's character?
- Are all of my relationships glorifying him?
- How about my integrity and work quality?
- Am I becoming more like Jesus Christ?

Knowing the purpose of your life, to glorify God, will help you make better decisions about how to live your life.

Psalm 86:12 says, "I will praise you, O Lord my God, with all my heart; I will glorify your name forever."

🌿 Glorify God in all of your workplace relationships.

SUMMARY OF PART FOUR

Relationships with Others

Key Points

41. Walk with the Wise: You will grow wise with the right friends and suffer harm with the wrong friends. Your friends will impact your success. Choose them wisely.

42. Respect Your Employer: When it comes to job performance give your employer full respect and consideration. Christian employees should be the best employees in every organization.

43. Dealing with a Fool: A fool is the opposite of a wise person, and most fools will self-destruct. Guard yourself against their folly but tell them about Jesus Christ when they are ready to hear.

44. Encourage One Another: An encourager is someone who stands by your side and calls you to move forward to a better place. Encourage your coworkers with your supportive words and personal actions.

45. Deborah's Leadership: Leaders are magnets, not bulldozers. They are subject-matter experts within their sphere of influence; they step forward when others don't. Leaders lead by example and are affirmed by their followers.

46. The Generous Worker: Generous people are free of smallness; they are magnanimous and not petty. Be generous and share your time, skills, and resources with others.

47. The Spirit of Edification: Christians are endowed with the spirit of edification. Affirm what is good in your employer and coworkers; support what is right and productive. Bring out the best in others.

48. Sanctified Ambition: Work hard and excel, but do not look down on others in the process. Be ambitious for your own success as well as the success of others.

49. Church and Work: What you learn and do on Sunday at church makes life better from Monday through Friday at work. Christian fellowship begins vertically with Jesus Christ and extends horizontally throughout his Body, the church.

50. Jealousy in the Workplace: The workplace is a breeding ground for jealousy. Jealousy goes hand-in-hand with hatred, discord, fits of rage, dissensions, and quarreling. Its consequences are always negative. Jealousy is worldly and not of God.

51. The Golden Rule: The golden rule is labeled "golden" because of its great value. It is applied Christianity for us as well as a universally admired life principle for others. Treat others as you would like to be treated.

52. Working to Give: Would you rather be known as a giver or a taker? Givers are appreciated and sought after. They are synergistic. Givers build organizations and contribute to the success of the people around them. Who wants to work with someone who only takes?

53. The Leader Who Empowers: The best leaders teach the teachable and then send them out to become leaders themselves. If God has blessed you with the ability to lead, use your gift to empower others.

54. The Office Enemy: Christians are not "eye for eye" people. Love your office enemy the same way Jesus loves your office enemy. Do your job, do it well, and pray for your enemies.

55. The Servant Leader: Jesus is the world's most successful servant leader. He came to serve and not be served. Servant leaders bring out the best in others. They build the people who build the organization.

56. Wolves at Work: There are some in the workplace who are actively anti-Christian. They have little use for Jesus Christ and, as one of his people, little use for you. Take the high road when responding to them, and do not mimic their destructive behavior.

57. Glorifying God at Work: God's glory is the manifestation of his presence. "Whatever you do, do it all for the glory of God," and this includes all of your workplace relationships and actions.

Key Verses

Proverbs 1:7b: Fools despise wisdom and discipline.

Proverbs 11:24–25: One man gives freely, yet gains even more; another withholds unduly, but comes to poverty. A generous man will prosper; he who refreshes others will himself be refreshed.

Proverbs 13:20: He who walks with the wise grows wise, but a companion of fools suffers harm.

Proverbs 18:2: A fool finds no pleasure in understanding but delights in airing his own opinions.

Matthew 5:38–39: "You have heard that it was said, 'Eye for eye, and tooth for tooth.' But I tell you, Do not resist an evil person. If someone strikes you on the right cheek, turn to him the other also."

Matthew 7:12: So in everything, do to others what you would have them do to you, for this sums up the Law and the Prophets.

Matthew 10:16: "I am sending you out like sheep among wolves. Therefore be as shrewd as snakes and as innocent as doves."

Luke 6:38: "Give, and it will be given to you. A good measure, pressed down, shaken together and running over, will be poured into your lap. For with the measure you use, it will be measured to you."

Acts 2:42: They devoted themselves to the apostles' teaching and to the fellowship, to the breaking of bread and to prayer.

Acts 20:35: In everything I did, I showed you that by this kind of hard work we must help the weak, remembering the words the Lord Jesus himself said: "It is more blessed to give than to receive."

1 Corinthians 3:3: You are still worldly. For since there is jealousy and quarreling among you, are you not worldly? Are you not acting like mere men?

1 Corinthians 10:30: So whether you eat or drink or whatever you do, do it all for the glory of God.

1 Corinthians 15:33: Do not be misled: "Bad company corrupts good character."

2 Corinthians 9:6: Remember this: Whoever sows sparingly will also reap sparingly, and whoever sows generously will also reap generously.

2 Corinthians 9:11: You will be made rich in every way so that you can be generous on every occasion, and through us your generosity will result in thanksgiving to God.

2 Corinthians 10:8: For even if I boast somewhat freely about the authority the Lord gave us for building you up rather than pulling you down, I will not be ashamed of it.

Ephesians 6:5: Slaves, obey your earthly masters with respect and fear, and with sincerity of heart, just as you would obey Christ.

Philippians 2:3–5: Do nothing out of selfish ambition or vain conceit, but in humility consider others better than yourselves. Each of you should look not only to your own interests, but also to the interests of others. Your attitude should be the same as that of Christ Jesus.

1 Timothy 6:1: All who are under the yoke of slavery should consider their masters worthy of full respect, so that God's name and our teaching may not be slandered.

1 Timothy 6:18: Command them to do good, to be rich in good deeds, and to be generous and willing to share.

Hebrews 3:13: But encourage one another daily, as long as it is called Today, so that none of you may be hardened by sin's deceitfulness.

1 Peter 2:18: Slaves, submit yourselves to your masters with all respect, not only to those who are good and considerate, but also to those who are harsh.

FOCUS QUESTIONS

Read Proverbs 13:20 and 1 Corinthians 15:33. Do you have any coworkers or customers who are people of "bad character?" How do you handle these relationships?

Workers always have something to say about the boss. As part of your Christian witness, how can you speak respectfully about your boss and other managers even if you disagree with their management style?

Deborah spoke with authority and led by example. In what areas of your job responsibilities can you speak with authority? In what ways are you setting the right example for others?

Give one or more examples of when you were generous with another person. What good things have happened, either to you or the other person, as a result of your generosity?

Think of some coworkers whom you can edify for their good work. When can you do this?

Read Philippians 2:3–5. When competing against others, how do you balance your own interests with the "interests of others"? What is the best way to respond when another person is successful (e.g., gets a promotion and you do not)?

Do you have Christian friends from your home church with whom you can share your career challenges? If not can you think of one or more to ask?

Have you ever been jealous of another person's career success? How did these jealous feelings impact your own work-life? What is the best way to deal with your jealousy of another person?

Read 2 Corinthians 9:6. Give an example of the law of sowing and reaping working in your work-life?

How does our culture misapply the Old Testament "eye for eye" law by using it as justification for more conflict? Give an example of when it would be best to turn the other cheek regarding a minor offense by another.

Think of others in the workplace whom you influence. What can you do to bring out the best in them and in the quality of their work?

Read Matthew 10:16. What does it mean for Christians to be "shrewd as snakes" yet "innocent as doves?"

We Christians are called to glorify God with the whole of our lives. What can you do to glorify God in your job and career?

PART FIVE

GOD'S WISDOM
AND WILL

58

THE PURPOSE OF LIFE

HOW CAN YOU evaluate the success of your life if you don't know the purpose of your life?

Success in the workplace is meaningful and important; but what about success across the full spectrum of life including family, friends, and community? What about your well-being, values, and relationship with God? Are people still successful if they are excelling at work yet failing God and others?

What's the standard?

The good news is God defines what is or is not a successful way to live. He literally wrote the book on successful living, and in 1 Corinthians 10:31 he declares, "Whatever you do, do it all for the glory of God."

The purpose of life is to glorify God.

This is why you were born. God calls you to glorify him in whatever you do. No matter what is going on in your life—in the easy times and in the difficult times, in joy or in sorrow, in wealth or in need—you "do it all for the glory of God."

The truly successful person knows God, obeys God, and glorifies him in every realm of life.

To glorify God is to manifest his character. Whether you are a trainee in a cubicle or at the top of your profession in a corner office, it's the same to God. Manifest his character and do all things his way.

Proverbs 3:6 says, "In all your ways acknowledge him."

The best way to glorify God is to be like his Son, Jesus.
Hebrews 1:3 declares, "The Son is the radiance of God's glory and the exact representation of his being."

Jesus tells us in John 15:8, "This is to my Father's glory, that you bear much fruit." God's fruit is always good fruit. Work hard, put in the hours, and achieve success in your career, but don't turn your back on the rest of God's creation or sell your soul in the process.

Life is bigger than your current job or your next promotion. Balance your life's priorities with an all-encompassing perspective that glorifies God.

In his book, *God at Work,* David Miller shares the following comments from a successful business professional who was reflecting on his career:

> I have worked hard to reach the pinnacle of my profession. I have more money than God, yet I am unfulfilled. My marriage is a shambles. I hardly know my kids, and when I look in the mirror, I wonder where the man went who so idealistically graduated from college thirty years ago and was ready to make his mark on the world.

This man doesn't know the purpose of his life. He thinks success in just one area of life—career—leads to success in every area. It doesn't. This man needs to correct his understanding of what it takes to live a successful life. He, just like all of us, needs Jesus Christ.

🌿 To glorify Jesus Christ in every realm of life is to be successful in every realm of life.

59

WISDOM THAT COMES
FROM HEAVEN

THE BEST WISDOM is the "wisdom that comes from heaven." It has God as its author, it carries God's point of view, and it never fails. God's wisdom will always point you in the right direction.

Most of us are quick to say, "Knowledge is power." But, the fact is, your knowledge is only potential power until you put it to wise use. Knowledge is about facts; wisdom is about the decisions you make with those facts—one complements the other, and both are needed.

Wisdom is the ability to judge correctly.

Your wisdom—for better or worse—is the extension of your knowledge. Wise people make good decisions, and they do well in life.

James 3:17 describes the "wisdom that comes from heaven."

> But the wisdom that comes from heaven is first of all pure; then peace-loving, considerate, submissive, full of mercy and good fruit, impartial and sincere.

The "wisdom that comes from heaven," the best wisdom, contains the following eight qualities.

First of all pure: Having pure motives is the first and primary characteristic of godly wisdom. To be pure is to be free of corruption. Do what is good and honorable throughout your workday. Follow an ethical career path. Proverbs 3:7 tells you to "shun evil."

Peace-loving: Seek unity within your organization. Restore any broken relationships with your coworkers. Mitigate strife. Lay aside revenge and resentment.

Considerate: Listen to and learn from your fellow stakeholders. Know how your individual actions affect others at your place of employment.

Submissive: God is never wrong and obedience to him is never a mistake. Stay true to your Christian values.

Mercy: Kindness, compassion, and benevolence are all Christlike qualities. The wise keep moving forward in life while the foolish waste their time holding grudges.

Good fruit: Careers span decades. They are like fruit because they take time to mature. Plan for the long haul. The wisest choices are the ones that bring the best results by the best means over the longest period of time.

Impartial: Go where the facts lead you. Operate in the realm of reason rather than emotion. Be free of prejudice.

Sincere: Truth and light will always win the day. Be free of deceit and free of hypocrisy. Choose transparency over deception.

🌿 Godly wisdom "yields better returns than gold." (Prov. 3:14)

GET WISDOM

GOD PLACES A premium on wisdom as stated in Proverbs 4:5–7: "Get wisdom, get understanding... she will protect you; love her, and she will watch over you. Wisdom is supreme; therefore get wisdom."

God's will for you is to "get wisdom."

His wisdom is supreme, which in the language of the Old Testament means it is the principal thing—it is first, chief, and primary—it is the beginning.

Proverbs 16:16 adds more when it proclaims, "How much better to get wisdom than gold," and Proverbs 3:13 says, "Blessed is the man who finds wisdom."

God knows you will need more wisdom at times, and this is why he gives you the promise of James 1:5–6.

"If any of you lacks wisdom, he should ask God, who gives generously to all without finding fault, and it will be given to him. But when he asks, he must believe and not doubt." Consider this passage in its various parts:

If any of you lacks wisdom. The "you" refers to Christians. This passage is God's promise to all Christians who recognize their need for more wisdom.

He should ask God. God will provide the wisdom you need to get you to the best answers to life's most important questions. Think of him first.

Who gives generously. God is not stingy with his wisdom. He gives liberally. There will be no lack in the wisdom he gives you.

God communicates his wisdom through the commandments, principles, and illustrations found in his Word; through the preaching and teaching at your local church; and through the counsel of other believers. The Holy Spirit can illuminate your thinking during times of prayer, reflection, or worship. Look for God's hand at work in a change in your circumstance. God can get his wisdom to you in many ways.

To all. All Christians are included in God's promise of more wisdom, not just a select few.

Without finding fault. God will give his wisdom to you without reproach. No condemnation. He is delighted that you turned to him in your time of need.

And it will be given to him. Expect to hear from God. Listen for his message.

But when he asks, he must believe and not doubt. Wisdom is God's promise, and your faith activates his promise. Faith is believing what God says is true while the world gives you reasons to doubt.

God will guide you by making you wise in his ways.

🌿 Ask God for more wisdom so you can make better decisions with your life.

61

WISDOM SPEAKS

PROVERBS 8 PERSONIFIES wisdom. It is written in such a way that if wisdom could talk, she ("wisdom" is feminine in the Hebrew) would be speaking directly to you.

The chapter opens with Proverbs 8:1 by asking, "Does not wisdom call out? Does not understanding raise her voice?"

In Proverbs 8:6–11 God's wisdom speaks and declares, "Listen, for I have worthy things to say; I open my lips to speak what is right. My mouth speaks what is true…All the words of my mouth are just…To the discerning all of them are right…for wisdom is more precious than rubies."

God's wisdom is worthy, right, true, just, and precious. She has good things to say to you, and she wants to be heard.

What are wisdom's promises? Proverbs 8:18–21 gives you the answer:

> "With me are *riches* and *honor, enduring wealth* and *prosperity*. My fruit is better than fine gold; what I yield surpasses choice silver. I walk in the way of righteousness, along the paths of justice, bestowing wealth on those who love me and making their *treasuries full*." (emphasis added)

When you let God's wisdom direct your life these five blessings are sure to follow:

Riches. These riches are God's guarantee of sufficiency in the world. He always provides for his faithful. God may provide just enough or much more than enough, but he will always provide ample bread and resources to those who live life his way.

Honor. Your God-centric wisdom will be noticed by your family, friends, and associates. You will be respected by others and will enjoy an honorable reputation.

Enduring wealth. Applying God's wisdom to your life yields "enduring wealth," which is your heavenly wealth. This wealth is durable and eternal. Trusting in God today will reap rewards in every tomorrow.

Prosperity. "Prosperity" here in the NIV is translated "righteousness" in the NASB and KJV. To be declared righteous by God is to be in right standing before God. The benefits of this right relationship are "better than fine gold," and they surpass "choice silver."

Full treasuries. The application of God's wisdom to your life will make your "treasuries full." Note that "treasuries" is plural. We believers possess two treasuries: a storehouse filled with God's provision and an armory filled with God's power.

Finally, Proverbs 8:35 is a promise to those who embrace God's wisdom: "For whoever finds me finds life and receives favor from the Lord."

The world has many voices speaking to you about your values. Mute the world, separate the flesh from the Spirit, and trust in God's wisdom.

🌿 God's wisdom is worthy, right, true, just, and precious.

FREEDOM WITHIN LIMITS

GOD GIVES YOU the freedom to pursue your personal preferences with your career. These preferences can involve things like where to work, what occupation to choose, or what to decide regarding any other important work-life option.

You are free to make these and any number of work-related choices so long as you honor God in the process. This principle of being free to pursue your personal preferences, while at the same time remaining obedient to God, can be referred to as "freedom within limits."

Free to eat fruit but not the apple

The Bible's first reference to freedom within limits occurs in the Garden of Eden and is recorded in Genesis 2:15–17: "The Lord God took the man and put him in the Garden of Eden to work it and take care of it. And the Lord God commanded the man, 'You are free to eat from any tree in the garden; but you must not eat from the tree of the knowledge of good and evil, for when you eat of it you will surely die.'"

What God is saying to Adam is the key to understanding freedom within limits: "You are free to eat from any tree in the garden [you are free to make choices and pursue your personal preferences]; but you must not eat from the tree of the knowledge of good and evil [but, your choices are limited by my other commandment]."

In this passage God is telling Adam to enjoy any fruit he likes (e.g., pears, oranges, or grapes), but he is to not eat the apple.

God is not limiting Adam's choices to only one option, and God will be equally pleased with any of Adam's choices so long as Adam does not "eat from the tree of the knowledge of good and evil," (i.e., the apple).

It is important to remember—and this is a key point—that God did this for Adam's own good.

God blessed Adam with a free will, but Adam's freedom had limits. All of mankind is blessed with this same free will along with its companion principle of always obeying God's already-revealed commandments.

Free to choose but freedom has its limits

In the realm of work, you are free to make any number of choices and to pursue many career options. But in areas like morality, honesty, and ethics, God's commandments must be obeyed.

For example, are you free to choose your place of employment? Yes. Are you free to choose your career specialty? Yes. Free to initiate a job change? Yes. But can you engage in an illegal business activity? No. Can you lie to a customer? No. Falsify your resume? No. God's commandments already address these types of choices, and he gave you his commandments for your own good.

2 Corinthians 3:17 says, "Now the Lord is the Spirit, and where the Spirit of the Lord is, there is freedom."

🌿 God gives you the freedom to pursue your personal preferences with your career.

63

FORGET THE FORMER THINGS

ISAIAH 43:18–19 ADDRESSES the principle of God asking his followers to "forget the former things" before he can bring in the new. Isaiah, the prophet, is speaking for God when he says:

> "Forget the former things; do not dwell on the past. See, I am doing a new thing! Now it springs up; do you not perceive it? I am making a way in the desert and streams in the wasteland."

The context of Isaiah 43:18–19 is God's message to the people of Israel regarding the coming of their Messiah, Jesus Christ. The spirit of God's message can be applied to your life now just as it was to the people of Israel's then.

Consider the passage in its three parts:

"Forget the former things; do not dwell on the past."

Are former things from your past holding you back (e.g., the wrong people, old conflicts, prior mistakes, flawed thinking)? We Christians can still get caught up in the former things that God wants us to forget. If you aren't careful, you can be controlled by things that Jesus already defeated at Calvary.

If this is you, "do not dwell on the past." Repent, ask for God's forgiveness, move forward, and dwell on the new things Christ has for you.

"See, I am doing a new thing! Now it springs up; do you not perceive it?"

Jesus Christ is the new thing in the life of every Christian. See his work in your life.

Second Corinthians 5:17 says, "Therefore, if anyone is in Christ, he is a new creation; the old has gone, the new has come!" Forget the old and receive the new.

If you are searching for the latest new thing to help you with the demands of your job, why not start by bringing Jesus to work with you every day? The world is full of all kinds of career advice. Some of it is good, but some is also frivolous and just trendy.

Jesus's ways are rock solid, timeless, and always correct.

Spend time with Jesus from Monday through Friday at work, just as you do on Sundays in church. Do your job while emulating Christ's character and obeying his Word.

"I am making a way in the desert and streams in the wasteland."

This last part of the Isaiah 43:18–19 passage tells you that God can make a way when you are in the "desert and…

wasteland." He can make a way where you do not see a way. He will give you direction and provision to get you out of any world-based desert. Ask Jesus to do the things that only he can do.

🌿 Forget the former things that are holding you back.

64

THE YIELDED LIFE

JESUS CHRIST IS the most influential person who ever lived. He is mankind's ultimate thought leader and agent for change. In John 14:6 Jesus declares, "I am the way and the truth and the life."

After changing the world over two thousand years ago, Jesus is still alive and well, and today over two billion people are following his teachings.

One key to Jesus's greatness is revealed in John 6:38: "For I have come down from heaven not to do my will but to do the will of him who sent me."

Jesus only did "the will of him who sent me," which is to say he always obeyed his Father. Jesus was perfect because he was perfectly obedient.

Jesus's life was a yielded life. He emphasizes this fact with his own words in these additional verses from the Gospel of John:

- "The Son can do nothing by himself." (John 5:19)

214

- "I do not accept praise from men." (John 5:41)
- "I am not here on my own." (John 7:28)
- "I am not seeking glory for myself." (John 8:50)
- "For I did not speak of my own accord." (John 12:49)
- "It is the Father…who is doing his work." (John 14:10)

Jesus completed all the work he was sent to do. He heard and followed his Father's voice. Jesus stayed focused despite the world's noise. He was always secure in his beliefs and decisive in his actions. Jesus never wavered, wasn't wishy-washy, and always made the right calls.

Just as Jesus yielded to his Father, you can yield to Jesus. When you consistently do his will, your life becomes more purposeful and productive. No situational ethics and no second-guessing of your decisions.

The yielded life is simple and uncomplicated.

Just do what God tells you to do and leave the rest to him.

Who better to be your workplace guide than Jesus Christ? He is the personification of greatness and every worker's perfect role model.

Colossians 1:15 says, "He is the image of the invisible God, the firstborn over all creation." Mirror his values and not the world's.

🌿 The yielded life produced good results for Jesus, and it will produce good results for you.

65

JOSHUA'S EARLY TRAINING

J OSHUA LED ISRAEL in the conquest of the Promised Land. He was a military commander, national leader, and great man in history. But long before his miraculous crossing of the Jordan River and victory at Jericho, God taught Joshua what he needed to know to become a godly leader.

Joshua's early training demonstrates how God can use your experiences to equip and prepare you before calling you to do greater works later in life.

Three of Joshua's early life experiences are recorded in the following Old Testament passages, all of which occur prior to Joshua becoming Israel's primary leader.

Exodus 33:11 tells us that as a young aide to Moses, Joshua met with God in the tent of meeting.

"Then Moses would return to the camp, but his young aide Joshua son of Nun did not leave the tent."

Joshua was proactive about spending one-on-one time with God. He did not rely exclusively on the counsel of men. Joshua learned early in his career that spending time with God brings an understanding of the will of God.

Exodus 17:8–16 reveals when Joshua learned that it is God who supplies the victory.

Excerpts from the passage read as follows: "So Joshua fought the Amalekites as Moses had ordered...As long as Moses held up his hands, the Israelites were winning, but whenever he lowered his hands, the Amalekites were winning."

The correlation between Moses's raised hands and Joshua's winning identifies God as the source of Israel's battlefield success. When fighting the battle, Joshua learned to depend on God's strength and not his own. Joshua suited up and engaged the Amalekites, and God supplied the victory.

Like he did with Joshua, God can work through you to bring a victory even when you are outnumbered by the enemy.

This last story which is recorded in Numbers 14:6–9 is about the twelve Israelites, including Joshua, who left their camp in the wilderness to explore the Promised Land. When they returned only Joshua and Caleb, a minority of two, believed in God and gave a faithful report to the assembly.

Numbers 14:5–9 declares, "Joshua son of Nun and Caleb... said to the entire Israelite assembly, 'The land we passed through and explored is exceedingly good...do not rebel against the Lord. And do not be afraid of the people of the land, because we will swallow them up. Their protection is gone, but the Lord is with us. Do not be afraid of them.'"

In this story Joshua learned that the consensus of his peer group could be very wrong about the things of God. Joshua believed in God's Word instead of the opinions of the masses. In the end God was right and the masses were wrong—God is always right.

🌿 God is teaching you through your experiences today while preparing you for greater things tomorrow.

JONATHAN'S FAITH

GOD CAN ACCOMPLISH his purposes through many or just a few. Jonathan speaks this truth in 1 Samuel 14:6: "Nothing can hinder the Lord from saving, whether by many or by few." Jonathan knows this to be true because he is one of God's few.

First Samuel 14:1–15 records how God took action through two faithful believers, Jonathan and his armor-bearer, when Israel's established leaders sat and did nothing.

Consider the following passages from 1 Samuel 14:1–15:

First Samuel 14:1–2: One day Jonathan son of Saul said to the young man bearing his armor, "Come, let's go over to the Philistine outpost on the other side." But he did not tell his father. Saul was staying on the outskirts of Gibeah under a pomegranate tree in Migron. With him were about six hundred men.

In an act of provocation toward Israel, the Philistines set up a military outpost near Israel's camp. The only response to this from Israel's leader, King Saul, was to sit "under a pomegranate tree" with his "six hundred men."

Saul had become a weak leader. He did nothing in the face of this enemy threat, but God did something. God raised up Saul's son, Jonathan, who summoned his armor-bearer and they took immediate action.

First Samuel 14:6: Jonathan said to his young armor-bearer, "Come, let's go over to the outpost of those uncircumcised fellows. Perhaps the Lord will act in our behalf."

Saul and Jonathan were facing the same crisis. But, Saul sat while Jonathan moved in faith.

There will be times in your life when God calls you to take action in a particular situation. He is always ready to use a faithful believer who will do his will. God can accomplish more with one or two who are faithful (e.g., Jonathan and his armor-bearer) than with a king and "six hundred men" who are not.

Jonathan approached the enemy camp while asking God for a sign.

First Samuel 14:8–9: Jonathan said, "Come, then; we will cross over toward the men and let them see us. If they say to us, 'Wait there until we come to you,' we will stay where we are and not go up to them. But if they say, 'Come up to us,' we will climb up, because that will be our sign that the Lord has given them into our hands.'"

God gave Jonathan the sign he asked for.

First Samuel 14:11–12: So both of them showed themselves to the Philistine outpost. "Look!" said the Philistines. "The Hebrews are crawling out of the holes they were hiding in." The men of the outpost shouted to Jonathan and his armor-bearer, "Come up to us and we'll teach you a lesson."

The Philistines' mocking of Israel was the very sign that initiated their destruction.

First Samuel 14:13: Jonathan climbed up, using his hands and feet, with his armor-bearer right behind him. The Philistines fell before Jonathan, and his armor-bearer followed and killed behind him.

God prevailed over his enemies through the hands of one faithful leader and his single follower. Long odds don't matter when you are fighting God's battles. God's paths to victory go beyond the natural.

First Samuel 14:15: Then panic struck the whole army—those in the camp and field, and those in the outposts and raiding parties—and the ground shook. It was a panic sent by God.

Jonathan's faith made the difference, and his actions opened the door to God's intervention. There is no limit to the things God can do to advance his will and purpose.

Remember Jonathan. He and his armor-bearer did more than a king and his six hundred men.

When threatened by an enemy, remain faithful, don't compromise your values, and keep moving forward.

🌿 "If God is for us, who can be against us?" (Rom. 8:31)

GOD'S WILL FOR THE WORKER

N O MATTER WHAT type of work you do, where you are working, or how long you have been at it, God's will for you and your daily labors includes the following:

God's will is for you to serve him with your work.

God designed you to work and to be fulfilled in that work. Human work is a divinely ordained activity reflecting the glory of God. Christian workers should be the best workers in every organization.

Colossians 3:24 declares, "It is the Lord Christ you are serving."

God can bring out the best in you in every workplace circumstance.

God's will is to bless you through your work.

Proverbs 14:23 declares, "All hard work brings a profit." God promises that work performed under his governance will always pay off—this is his will for the fruits of your labor.

God uses your work to provide for your "daily bread"—the necessities of life such as food, shelter, and clothing, which Jesus refers to in the Lord's Prayer in Matthew 6:11.

Whether you actually grow the food, build the shelter, and make the clothes, or your labor provides the income to buy these things, God is the Giver of the talents and resources used to acquire your "daily bread."

Proverbs 8:18 says, "With me are riches and honor, enduring wealth and prosperity." Your honorable work will always bring a reward to God, self, and others—no matter what.

God's will is for you to grow through your workplace trials.

Trials come with every job. They are inevitable. However, God can use your trials to get your attention about things you would not otherwise address.

James 1:12 declares, "Blessed is the man who perseveres under trial."

Don't waste your trials—grow through your next trial and learn something new from it.

God's will is for you to be his witness in the workplace.

Jesus says in Matthew 5:13–14, "You are the salt of the earth… You are the light of the world." As a Christian in the workplace, you are salt that inhibits decay and light that dispels the darkness. All Christians are evangelists, and the workplace is our mission field.

🌿 Honorable work is God's idea.

DECISION MAKING GOD'S WAY

Do you want to make decisions that are consistent with God's will? No second-guessing. No looking back. No uncertainty.

You can by following these three steps for making decisions God's way:

Where God's Word commands, always obey.

This first and most basic principle is your starting point for making better decisions. Begin by knowing God's Word, understanding its context, and being obedient to what it says. Doing what the Bible tells you to do is always the best choice.

Philippians 4:7 promises that when you obey God's Word, you will enjoy "the peace of God, which transcends all understanding."

Should you falsify a work document? Deceive a customer? Steal from a coworker? God's Word speaks to these types of choices and his Word is clear: do none of these things. These types of decisions are simple and straight forward.

Where God's Word has no command, you are free to choose.

What do you do in a situation where God's Word has no specific command (i.e., a noncommandment decision)?

For example, should you work for Company A or Company B? If the Bible commanded "always work for Company A," your decision would be clear cut (as in the first step), but the Bible never says this. How do you decide between the two companies?

Garry Friesen explores these types of decisions in his book, *Decision Making and the Will of God*, and he says the key to making a noncommandment decision is to know that God gives you the freedom and responsibility to make good choices.

God allows you to do your own investigation, fact-finding, and due diligence. You can look at the facts, press into God (through prayer, scriptural principles, godly counsel, etc.), make your decision, and move forward in a way that glorifies him.

The core issue in noncommandment decision making (e.g., should you work for Company A or Company B?), is to know that God will be pleased with either choice so long as you respect and honor him throughout the whole decision making process.

Developing the ability to make good noncommandment decisions is rooted in your personal relationship with Jesus Christ.

Trust the results of your decision to God's grace.

Your decision may result in quick success, or even a trial, but God remains active, involved, and in charge no matter what happens.

Isaiah 26:3 says, "You will keep in perfect peace him whose mind is steadfast, because he trusts in you."

❧ Obey God and trust your decisions to his grace.

69

THE PROBLEM WITH SELF-ESTEEM

COMMON SENSE TELLS us that high self-esteem is a must for thriving in the workplace. If you want to get ahead, you must feel good about yourself. Most of us have plenty to feel good about, too: our accomplishments, skills, influence, reputation, responsibilities, education, and more.

Taking pride in your career and the goods or services you produce are always good things, right? If this is true, what is God saying in Proverbs 16:18 when he proclaims, "Pride goes before destruction, a haughty spirit before a fall?"

This verse is a warning, and God wrote it for your own good. He does not want you to get hurt by putting too much stock in manufactured self-esteem or man-centered self-inflation.

In truth we tend to embrace our own high self-esteem while being repelled by the pride in others. Is there a difference? Perhaps, but it mostly depends on who is judging whom.

"Pride" used in Proverbs 16:18 means arrogance as characterized by majesty, pomp, and exaltation. Self-esteem can become a euphemism for pride, and this is the problem.

Pride is deceptive, personal, and a matter of degree. We can all pick out the prideful coworker, but can we see the pride in our own conduct? Jesus's words in Luke 4:23 come to mind: "Physician, heal yourself!"

Pride exalts the wrong person.

Pride takes over when the "self" in self-esteem takes center stage. Pride leaves no room for God. It pushes God off of his throne in your life and replaces him with your "self."

There is a point where a healthy self-image—a good thing—crosses the line to become tainted with pride, and God knows where the line is for each of us.

The Bible tells us more about pride in James 4:6: "God opposes the proud but gives grace to the humble." Think about it: "God opposes the proud." When you get full of yourself, God begins to oppose you. Your pride not only alienates your coworkers, but your pride alienates God, and neither of these consequences is desirable.

Humble yourself.

Keep your pride in check by applying James 4:10: "Humble yourselves before the Lord, and he will lift you up." John says something similar when talking about his relationship with Jesus in John 3:30: "He must become greater; I must become less."

🌿 Balance your high self-esteem with respect for God and others.

70

ZACCHAEUS'S SALVATION STORY

ZACCHAEUS IS DESCRIBED in Luke 19:1–10 as "a chief tax collector" who was wealthy. Yet, his big job, prestige, and money left him unfulfilled. Zacchaeus had the world, but still needed Jesus—he was a seeker on a spiritual journey.

Zacchaeus's salvation story is recorded in Luke 19:1–10:

Jesus entered Jericho and was passing through. A man was there by the name of Zacchaeus; he was a chief tax collector and was wealthy. He wanted to see who Jesus was, but being a short man he could not, because of the crowd. So he ran ahead and climbed a sycamore-fig tree to see him, since Jesus was coming that way.

When Jesus reached the spot, he looked up and said to him, "Zacchaeus, come down immediately. I must stay at your house today." So he came down at once and welcomed him gladly.

All the people saw this and began to mutter, "He has gone to be the guest of a 'sinner.'" But Zacchaeus stood up and said to the Lord, "Look, Lord! Here and now I give half of my possessions to the poor, and if I have cheated anybody out of anything, I will pay back four times the amount." Jesus said to him, "Today salvation has come to this house, because this man, too, is a son of Abraham. For the Son of Man came to seek and to save what was lost."

Zacchaeus's story demonstrates the following truths about salvation and the Christian experience:

Jesus Christ can be found by everyone who seeks him.

Zacchaeus is the only person in the story who "wanted to see who Jesus was," and he quickly found him. Isaiah 55:6 says, "Seek the Lord while he may be found; call on him while he is near."

Jesus is never far away from those who truly want to find him.

The "crowd" will hinder Jesus's work in your life.

Zacchaeus had to separate from the crowd because they were blocking his view of Jesus. He had to climb the tree and get above the others before he could see his Savior.

Zacchaeus, a repenting sinner, took the initiative to have an unobstructed view of Jesus.

Later, the same crowd "began to mutter" about what they had seen. They voiced contempt for both Jesus and Zacchaeus. Do not expect the world to affirm your Savior or your salvation. The crowd only saw a sinner, but Jesus saw a redeemed saint and friend.

Only Christians can have fellowship with Jesus Christ.

Jesus called Zacchaeus by name, and then said, "I must stay at your house today." Jesus called and saved Zacchaeus and then began a personal relationship with him.

Salvation in Christ is the antecedent to fellowship with Christ.

Christians are instruments for God's noble purposes.

Jesus did not require Zacchaeus to "give half of [his] possessions to the poor," nor that he "pay back four times" to anyone he had cheated. Zacchaeus alone decided to do these things. These good works were the fruit of his salvation. They were self-initiated acts of restoration and grace by a new Christian.

Zacchaeus didn't do these things to *get* saved—he did them *because* he was saved.

The final verse of the passage is as true for mankind today as it was for Zacchaeus back then. It is a summary of the gospel message. Jesus says in Luke 19:10, "For the Son of Man came to seek and to save what was lost."

🌿 Jesus can always be found by those who are seeking him.

SUMMARY OF PART FIVE

God's Wisdom and Will

Key Principles

58. The Purpose of Life: The purpose of life is to glorify God. The truly successful person knows God, obeys God, and glorifies him in every realm of life. Success in just one area of life (i.e., career) does not equate to success in every area of life.

59. Wisdom That Comes From Heaven: The best wisdom "comes from heaven." It has God as its author, it carries God's point of view, and it never fails. God's wisdom will always point you in the right direction.

60. Get Wisdom: God can get his wisdom to you in many ways: through the commandments, principles, and illustrations found in his Word; through the preaching and teaching at your local church; through the counsel of other believers; and through the illumination of the Holy Spirit in times of prayer, reflection, or worship.

61. Wisdom Speaks: God's wisdom is worthy, right, true, just, and precious. She ("wisdom" is feminine in the Hebrew) yields riches, honor, enduring wealth and prosperity.

62. Freedom within Limits: God has blessed you with the liberty to make wise choices in your life. You are free to pursue your personal preferences and to make any number of good choices so long as you honor God in the process.

63. Forget the Former Things: We Christians can get caught up in the "former things" that God wants us to forget. Keep moving forward and dwell on the new things Jesus Christ brings into your life.

64. The Yielded Life: Jesus was perfectly obedient to his Father, and his life was a yielded life. Just as Jesus yielded to his Father, you can yield to Jesus. The yielded life produced good results for Jesus, and it will produce good results for you.

65. Joshua's Early Training: God has been teaching and growing you through your life experiences—the blessings and the trials. He is preparing you for greater things to come.

66. Jonathan's Faith: God can accomplish his purposes through many or just a few. The odds do not make any difference when you are fighting on God's side.

67. God's Will for the Worker: God is always for you and never against you. Manifest his character in your work-life. Serve God with your work and grow through your workplace trials.

68. Decision Making God's Way: Where God's Word commands, always obey. Where God's Word has no command, you are free to choose. Trust the results of your decisions to God's grace and sovereignty.

69. The Problem with Self-Esteem: God does not want you to get hurt by putting too much stock in manufactured self-esteem or man-centered self-inflation. God "opposes the proud."

70. Zacchaeus's Salvation Story: Everyone needs Christ, and he can always be found by those who seek him. Do not expect the world to affirm your salvation or your Savior. We Christians are instruments for God's noble purposes.

Key Verses

Genesis 2:15–17: The Lord God took the man and put him in the Garden of Eden to work it and take care of it. And the Lord God commanded the man, "You are free to eat from any tree in the garden; but you must not eat from the tree of the knowledge of good and evil, for when you eat of it you will surely die."

Numbers 14:6–7: Joshua son of Nun and Caleb…said to the entire Israelite assembly, "The land we passed through and explored is exceedingly good."

1 Samuel 14:6b: Nothing can hinder the Lord from saving, whether by many or by few.

Proverbs 4:5–7a: Get wisdom, get understanding…she will protect you; love her, and she will watch over you. Wisdom is supreme; therefore get wisdom.

Proverbs 8:6–11: Listen, for I have worthy things to say; I open my lips to speak what is right. My mouth speaks what is true…

All the words of my mouth are just...To the discerning all of them are right...for wisdom is more precious than rubies, and nothing you desire can compare with her.

Proverbs 16:18: Pride goes before destruction, a haughty spirit before a fall.

Isaiah 26:3: You will keep in perfect peace him whose mind is steadfast, because he trusts in you.

Isaiah 43:18–19: Forget the former things; do not dwell on the past. See, I am doing a new thing! Now it springs up; do you not perceive it? I am making a way in the desert and streams in the wasteland.

Luke 19:1–4: Jesus entered Jericho and was passing through. A man was there by the name of Zacchaeus; he was a chief tax collector and was wealthy. He wanted to see who Jesus was, but being a short man he could not, because of the crowd. So he ran ahead and climbed a sycamore-fig tree to see him, since Jesus was coming that way.

John 6:38: "For I have come down from heaven not to do my will but to do the will of him who sent me."

1 Corinthians 10:31b: Whatever you do, do it all for the glory of God.

James 1:5–6a: If any of you lacks wisdom, he should ask God, who gives generously to all without finding fault, and it will be given to him. But when he asks, he must believe and not doubt.

James 3:17: But the wisdom that comes from heaven is first of all pure; then peace-loving, considerate, submissive, full of mercy and good fruit, impartial and sincere.

James 4:6a: God opposes the proud but gives grace to the humble.

FOCUS QUESTIONS

Read 1 Corinthians 10:31b. What does it mean to glorify God in whatever you do?

Think of someone you know or someone on the national stage who excelled at their career yet failed God, family, or others. Are they a successful person?

Proverbs 4:7 says, "Wisdom is supreme." What is wisdom? How does wisdom differ from knowledge? How is wisdom the extension of knowledge?

Like most of us, you have probably invested a lifetime in acquiring knowledge. What can you begin doing today to acquire more of God's wisdom?

What does the phrase "freedom within limits" mean to you?

Read Isaiah 43:18–19. Are things from your past holding you back (e.g., the wrong people, old conflicts, prior mistakes)? What former things do you need to leave behind so you can begin experiencing a new and better life today?

Jesus says in John 5:41, "I do not accept praise from men." Why should you be cautious about accepting too much praise from the world?

Give an example of how God prepared you in advance before giving you the opportunity to do a greater work at a later date.

In Samuel 14:1–15 Jonathan and his armor-bearer took action while Saul and his six hundred men sat and did nothing. Are you facing a challenge at work where the odds are against you? If so, how do you plan to address this challenge?

Are there times in your workday when it would be easy to compromise God's Word and take an unethical shortcut? How do you handle these temptations?

When did you receive Jesus Christ? Share your salvation story.

What are some of your favorite Bible verses? How can you apply them to your work-life?

PART SIX

WORK AS MINISTRY

71

WORK AS MINISTRY

W HEN YOU SHOW up to work, Jesus Christ shows up to work. You don't have to quit your job to be in full-time Christian service to God and others.

The following principles highlight the spiritual aspects of your daily labor. They are in no special order.

All Christians are equal.

When it comes to the things of God, it's Jesus Christ and then everyone else. There is no hierarchy of holiness in the New Testament church—no veneration of one class of believer over another.

All Christians are ministers of the Gospel, serving the same God in a variety of ways and in a variety of places. As a workplace Christian, you are a full-time minister of the Gospel of Jesus Christ at your place of employment.

Work is a calling from God.

Genesis 1 and 2 make it clear that human work is a divinely ordained activity. Your work has a spiritual dimension at its center, and it pleases God.

Work is not a curse, never has been and never will be. Work was good from the beginning, and it is still good today.

The true value of your work is not a matter of just dollars and cents.

Serve God and others with your work.

Ephesians 6:7 instructs you to "serve wholeheartedly, as if you were serving the Lord, not men."

Serving God and others with your work is ministering to God and others with your work. The translation of "minister" in the New Testament is "to serve or servant." First Peter 4:10 declares, "Each one should use whatever gift he has received to serve others."

The workplace is your mission field.

Believers are Christ's ambassadors to the workplace (2 Cor. 5:20), and we are God's salt and light to our coworkers (Matt. 5:13–14).

In John 17:15 Jesus prayed that we Christians not be taken out of the world. The verse reads, "My prayer is not that you take them out of the world." Jesus wants you to stay in the world just like he was in the world, and today few places are more worldly than the realm of work.

God has work for you to do here and now at your place of employment.

🌿 You are a full-time minister of the Gospel of Jesus Christ in your workplace.

YOUR WORK IS YOUR WITNESS

AVE YOU EVER asked yourself the question, "How can I be an effective witness to Christ in my workplace?"

In Titus 2:9–10 Paul describes one way to witness to your coworkers and managers, and it is through the excellence of your job performance. Paul's message is to let your work be your witness and his words are succinct and practical.

> Teach slaves to be subject to their masters in everything, to try to please them, not to talk back to them, and not to steal from them, but to show that they can be fully trusted, so that in every way they will make the teaching about God our Savior attractive.

In its historical context, this passage speaks of slaves and the work they do for their masters. "Slaves" is translated "servants" in the KJV. Some of these servants held high-ranking positions in their masters' households and many were Christians and local church members.

In today's culture the words "slave" and "master" can be loosely replaced with "employee" and "employer."

Titus 2:9–10 reveals the following keys to using your workplace demeanor and individual job performance as part of your Christian witness to others.

"Be subject to their masters in everything"

Do the job you were hired to do and do it well. Do it willingly even if your boss or circumstances are difficult. Do everything that is required in your job responsibilities, but, of course, you do not have to do anything illegal, immoral, or against God's Word.

"Try to please them"

Fulfill your job responsibilities while being agreeable, timely, and professional.

"Not to talk back to them"

Guard your tongue. Do not undermine the work product of your organization—no destructive agendas or malicious talk. Instead, contribute your ideas, add value, and engage in constructive dialogue. Cooperate with your managers and be a team player.

"And not to steal from them"

Give a full day's work for a full day's pay. Be honest in your dealings with others.

"But to show that they can be fully trusted"

Be reliable and steadfast. Keep your promises. Do such a good job that your employer will want to give you a key to the building and a promotion.

Titus 2:9–10 is not a man-made list of dos and don'ts. The keys in the passage have a divine purpose which is stated at the end of verse 10: "So that in every way they will make the teaching about God our Savior attractive."

Good and honorable work exalts Christ and his teachings. The way you handle your job responsibilities will make Jesus Christ "attractive" to those who do not know him.

🌿 Your exemplary work ethic is a witness to others.

73

LESSONS FROM PAUL'S CONVERSION

PAUL WAS ADVANTAGED, intelligent, and well-educated. He had every reason to embrace Jesus but chose to oppose him. In Galatians 1:13, Paul confesses, "I persecuted the church of God and tried to destroy it."

A few years later, Paul describes his presalvation self in Philippians 3:5–6: "A Hebrew of Hebrews; in regard to the law, a Pharisee; as for zeal, persecuting the church; as for legalistic righteousness, faultless."

Even a combative, anti-Christian like Paul ultimately accepted Jesus Christ. Paul's conversion story, found in Acts 9:1–31, reveals the following important lessons for today's Christian:

Paul was at his worst when he accepted Christ.

"Meanwhile, Saul was still breathing out murderous threats against the Lord's disciples. He went to the high priest and asked him for letters to the synagogues in Damascus, so that if he found any there who belonged to the Way, whether men or women, he might take them as prisoners to Jerusalem." (Acts 9:1–2)

Saul was Paul's Jewish name. He was "breathing out murderous threats against the Lord's disciples," which translates in the original Greek as "heaving with rage" toward Christ and his followers.

Jesus says in John 15:25, "They hated me without reason."

No person, no matter how lost, is beyond the reach of Jesus Christ. The most anti-Christian person you work with may be the very one who is closest to accepting Jesus. What, on the outside, is rejection of Christ may be the result of Spirit-led conviction on the inside.

Don't give up on the lost in your midst. Remain faithful and exercise discernment as you witness to your coworkers and others. Paul's conversion demonstrates the power of Jesus to change all lives for the better, even the most radical.

Paul was converted on a roadside, not in a church.

Acts 9:3 says that Paul accepted Christ "As he neared Damascus on his journey." The work of leading others to Christ is not confined to professional clergy and church services.

Jesus was a marketplace minister and so are you. Any person can receive Jesus Christ anywhere, anytime, and in any circumstance. Second Corinthians 6:2 says, "Now is the day of salvation."

Paul's conversion was unexpected.

Acts 9:26 tells us, "When he came to Jerusalem, he tried to join the disciples, but they were all afraid of him, not believing that he really was a disciple."

Jesus's disciples in Jerusalem were skeptical of Paul's salvation at first. In the eyes of some, Paul was a most unlikely candidate for conversion, but not so with God.

God's ways defy the world, and he is full of surprises. Remember that Paul did not convert himself nor did another person. The Holy Spirit converted Paul. God can do the unexpected—his ways are other-worldly and supernatural.

Paul became an evangelist for Jesus Christ.

Paul went from speaking murderous, anti-Christian threats in Acts 9:1 to preaching the Gospel of Jesus Christ in Acts 9:20: "At once he began to preach in the synagogues that Jesus is the Son of God."

🌿 No person is beyond the reach of Jesus Christ.

74

BRINGING GOOD NEWS TO WORK

ALL CHRISTIANS ARE evangelists. Jesus tells us this in Mark 16:15: "Go into all the world and preach the good news to all creation." As a Christian with a job, your place of employment is part of "all the world...all creation."

Your message is one of good news and glad tidings.

Jesus is both the Evangelist and the Good News. Luke 4:18–19 records the story of Jesus's return to his hometown of Nazareth where he announced the purpose of his ministry this way:

> "The Spirit of the Lord is on me, because he has anointed me to preach *good news* to the poor. He has sent me to proclaim *freedom* for the prisoners and *recovery* of sight for the blind, to *release* the oppressed, to proclaim the year of the Lord's *favor*." (emphasis added)

Note the words Jesus uses to describe his ministry: "good news...freedom...recovery...release...favor."

Jesus evangelized his former neighbors with good news, not with condemnation, scare tactics, or doom.

To "preach good news" is translated from the Greek word *euaggelizo,* which is the root of the English word, "evangelize." To evangelize is to announce the Messiah. The NKJV translates the same word in Luke 8:1 as "bringing the glad tidings."

Your ministry in the workplace is not to condemn your coworkers but to bring the good news and glad tidings of Jesus Christ.

The ministry of reconciliation

Second Corinthians 5:18–20 describes your ministry this way:

> All this is from God, who reconciled us to himself through Christ and gave us the *ministry of reconciliation*: that God was reconciling the world to himself in Christ, not counting men's sins against them. And he has committed to us the message of reconciliation. We are therefore Christ's ambassadors, as though God were making his appeal through us. (emphasis added)

God gave us the ministry of reconciliation with a message of reconciliation, and he is making his appeal to others through us.

You have already heard the good news, been reconciled to Christ, and are experiencing his blessings. As one of Christ's ambassadors to the workplace, you are the spokesperson of the sovereign whom you represent, i.e., Jesus Christ.

Your ministry is reconciliation and your message is good news to those who do not know Jesus Christ.

🌿 "How beautiful are the feet of those who bring good news!" (Rom. 10:15)

75

SERVING GOD FULL TIME

WHEN IT COMES to the things of God, it is Jesus Christ and then everyone else.

John 15:4 says we are all branches of the same vine (i.e., Jesus). Ephesians 1:3 declares that because of Jesus's work at Calvary, all believers are blessed with every spiritual blessing.

First Peter 2:9 says we are "a chosen people, a royal priest-hood, a holy nation, a people belonging to God, that you may declare the praises of him who called you out of darkness into his wonderful light."

Every believer is equipped to declare the praises of Jesus Christ. First Peter 2:5 proclaims that all of us are living stones building the same spiritual house.

As a Christian who goes to a job from Monday through Friday, you are a full-time minister of the Gospel of Jesus Christ in the workplace. When you go to work, you are following Jesus's example. Your work is full-time Kingdom work.

The fact is you do not have to quit your job in order to serve God because you are already serving him with, and through, your job and career.

No sacred-secular divide

Much of the confusion about what qualifies as bona fide service to God stems from early religious teachings that exalted clerical professionals as spiritually superior to everyday working believers. This two-tier, sacred-secular divide is not what God intends for his Body. In God's eyes all Christians share the same imputed righteousness of Christ; there is no sacred-secular divide, and there are no first- or second-class Christians.

Yes, some Christians do a much better job of serving Christ than others, but Jesus does not rank us by our vocations.

Of course, we respect and support the Lord's prophets, evangelists, apostles, pastors, and teachers (Eph. 4:11–12), and they are "worthy of double honor" for their work (1 Tim. 5:17). But most of them will be quick to tell you that Christian ministry is not limited to their specific callings.

Jesus is the church's only Shepherd, and all of us are his sheep—it's Jesus Christ first and then the rest of us who serve him.

Do you want to be a minister of the Gospel? Serve God full time? Change the world for Jesus Christ? Then start with the people who are in the place where you spend most of your time—your workplace.

🍃 All Christians are equipped to declare the praises of Jesus Christ.

76

PETER'S TRANSFORMATION

GOD CHANGED PETER from a common fisherman to an anointed miracle worker and apostle. Peter was a great Christian, but for all his greatness, Peter's faith journey was punctuated with episodes of doubt and struggle. God stayed with Peter step-by-step and transformed him from a new convert to a mature believer.

God transformed Peter, and he can do the same for you.

Peter was a common fisherman.

The Bible's first mention of Peter is in Matthew 4, which describes him as a fisherman in Galilee. Peter was casting a net into the lake when Jesus approached him and issued an invitation. Matthew 4:19–20 records the moment: "'Come, follow me,' Jesus said, 'and I will make you fishers of men.' At once they left their nets and followed him."

Peter was called by Christ in the midst of his daily labor—his was a workplace conversion.

Peter was ready to meet God as evidenced by his decision to leave his nets "at once." There was no coaxing, no pressure, and no theological discussions.

Peter struggled with his faith.

All of us have struggled with our faith, and Peter was no different.

For example, Satan targeted Peter in Caesarea Philippi and misled him regarding one of Jesus's teachings. Mark 8:32 records that Peter was so deceived by Satan that "Peter took him [Jesus] aside and began to rebuke him."

Peter, the great apostle, rebuked Jesus face-to-face. Jesus's response to Peter follows immediately in Mark 8:33: "But when Jesus turned and looked at his disciples, he rebuked Peter. 'Get behind me, Satan' he said. 'You do not have in mind the things of God, but the things of men.'"

Peter was one of only two disciples whom Jesus rebuked; the other was Judas. Judas ultimately betrayed Jesus, but Peter became his apostle.

Mark 14 gives another example of Peter's faith struggle. Mark 14:43–65 describes how Jesus was arrested by the Roman guards and taken before the Sanhedrin where he was beaten and condemned. Peter was in the courtyard outside when he was identified as a disciple of Jesus. In Mark 14:71, when confronted by the crowd, Peter denied that he knew Jesus: "He swore to them, 'I don't know this man you're talking about.'"

God still used Peter.

God never gave up on Peter, and he accomplished many things through Peter's new and born-again life. Here are three examples:

First, after Christ's Ascension and after the outpouring of the Holy Spirit at Pentecost, Peter ministered in Jerusalem. He preached his first sermon, and Acts 2:41 tells us, "Those who accepted his message were baptized, and about three thousand were added to their number that day."

Three thousand new Christians were brought into the Kingdom through the ministry of a man who less than two months earlier denied that he even knew Christ.

Second, a few days later, Acts 3:6 records Peter's healing of a crippled beggar at the temple gate: "Then Peter said, 'Silver or gold I do not have, but what I have I give you. In the name of Jesus Christ of Nazareth, walk.'"

The man got up and walked.

Third, in Acts 9:40 God used Peter in Joppa to raise Tabitha from the dead: "Peter sent them all out of the room; then he got down on his knees and prayed. Turning toward the dead woman, he said, 'Tabitha, get up.' She opened her eyes, and seeing Peter she sat up."

God did all of this through a recently converted fisherman who struggled with his faith. The God who used Peter can do the same with every other believer.

🌿 God can accomplish great things through you regardless of your background or personal struggles.

77

BRINGING GOD TO WORK

THERE WAS A period in Jesus's life when he worked as a young carpenter. This was after visiting the temple with his parents at age twelve (Luke 2:42) and before beginning his public ministry at age thirty (Luke 3:23).

Jesus grew in wisdom and stature.

We only have a few details about these years, but the Bible does tell us this much in Luke 2:52: "And Jesus grew in wisdom and stature, and in favor with God and men."

Jesus used his early work years to do more than labor as a carpenter. While working at his trade, Jesus submitted to his Father, and his Father shaped and blessed him. While working as a carpenter, Jesus "grew in wisdom and stature," according to his Father's will.

All workers can grow their work skills while on the job, but Christian workers can also grow in Christ through their work-life experiences.

In reality most on-the-job issues are basic life issues such as success or failure, pride or humility, peace or turmoil, forgiveness or resentment, and faith or fear. What better way to experience Christianity in action than through your work-life?

God can touch and change you just as profoundly from Monday through Friday in the workplace as he can on Sunday in church. God is doing his work in you while you are doing your work in the world.

Jesus affirmed the worth and dignity of human work.

If any person could have been exempted from work, it would have been Jesus. He is the King of Kings, yet he worked in his community like the rest of us. Why? Jesus did this to affirm the worth and dignity of human work. Jesus worked as an example for you to follow.

In Mark 6:3, when Jesus went back to preach in his hometown of Nazareth at the beginning of his public ministry, his former neighbors asked, "Isn't this the carpenter?" Jesus's neighbors didn't ask if he was a theologian or priest or scholar? No, they remembered Jesus by his occupation.

Jesus had the image and reputation of a working man. He was God incarnate, but they only saw the carpenter.

Many see you only through the lens of your occupation when in fact you bring the presence of Jesus Christ wherever you go. First Corinthians 3:16 says it well: "Don't you know that you yourselves are God's temple and that God's Spirit lives in you?"

Don't buy into the false premise that your faith has little relevance to your job. This separation of faith and work is a man-made concept. Bringing God to work is the best career decision you will ever make.

🌿 The centrality of Christ encompasses all things, including your job and career.

GOOD WORKS IN THE WORKPLACE

D O YOU HAVE a reputation for doing good works? Are they a regular part of your work week, and if they are, why?

As Christians we don't do good works to *get* saved—we do good works *because* we are saved. A good work is a free and voluntary act of service for another person. Doing good works is the fruit of your salvation in Jesus Christ.

Created to do good works

Ephesians 2:10 addresses the issue of Christians doing good works:

For we are God's workmanship, created in Christ Jesus to do good works, which God prepared in advance for us to do.

Ephesians 2:10 begins by telling us who we are. "For we are God's workmanship, created in Christ Jesus." The "we" refers to Christians, and our new lives are the result of "God's workmanship." God has changed us into something different from what we were before.

God is the Master Worker; we are the product of his workmanship, and now he is using us for his purposes. Every person is created, but only Christians are re-created in Christ Jesus. We are new, transformed, and born again.

Why did God save us? Keeping within the context of Ephesians 2:10, God saved us to "do good works." Doing good works for others is a part of your new lifestyle.

Titus 2:14 (KJV) describes us as "a peculiar people, zealous of good works." We Christians are peculiar in that we are distinctive. We stand out from the crowds. We are zealous for good works that go beyond society's norms.

Good works prepared in advance

Your calling to do good works for others is clear, but the correct application of this calling will require some wisdom.

For example, you can freely share your professional knowledge with a coworker, cover for someone at lunch so they can run an errand, or help another person operate a piece of equipment. All this is easy enough, but how about the low-performing worker with a bad attitude? Do you rescue them with your good works? Maybe—maybe not.

We are not called to do every possible good work everywhere and at all times. Ephesians 2:10 is telling us to only do the good works that "God prepared in advance for us to do."

Exercise discernment in the application of Ephesians 2:10. Your good works are customized to the circumstances and many will be Spirit-led divine appointments.

Finally, glorify Jesus Christ with your good works and not yourself. Jesus declares in Matthew 5:16, "In the same way, let your light shine before men, that they may see your good deeds and praise your Father in heaven."

🌿 Be zealous for good works that go beyond society's norms.

79

HUMILITY IN THE WORKPLACE

PROVERBS 22:4 PROMISES that "humility and the fear of the Lord bring wealth and honor and life." Maintaining a lifestyle of biblical humility brings glory to God as well as "wealth and honor" to you. James 4:10 says, "Humble yourselves before the Lord, and he will lift you up."

Humility is the highest virtue.

Biblical humility is simply recognizing your dependence on God. Andrew Murray, in his classic book *Humility* says, "Humility is the highest virtue of a human being. In fact it is the root of every virtue."

If you are humble, you are in very good company. Numbers 12:3 proclaims, "Now Moses was a very humble man, more humble than anyone else on the face of the earth." Moses was a man of historic achievement. The books of Exodus, Leviticus, Numbers and Deuteronomy record the amazing things God did through him. Moses was a very humble man yet a great man.

His life demonstrates that great humility goes hand in hand with great accomplishment.

Humility is never about denying your talents or successes. Humble people are simply more God-centered and other-people-centered than they are self-centered.

Some in the world turn the definition of humility upside down and make it synonymous with weakness, inferiority, and even self-abasement. Don't believe them. They do not understand humility, but we will love them just the same.

Humility exalts God, while pride, the opposite of humility, exalts self.

He who humbles himself will be exalted.

Consider Luke 14 which records Jesus's parable concerning the humble. The setting of the parable is a Sabbath dinner at the home of a prominent Pharisee. The Pharisee and his guests were the movers and shakers of the community. They were affluent, well-educated, and influential—the social and religious elites of their time.

Jesus seized the opportunity, and his message to them is recorded in Luke 14:7–10:

When he [Jesus] noticed how the guests picked the places of honor at the table, he told them this parable: "When someone invites you to a wedding feast, do not take the place of honor, for a person more distinguished than you may have been invited. If so, the host who invited both of you will come and say to you, 'Give this man your seat.' Then, humiliated, you will have to take the least important place. But when you are invited, take the lowest place, so that when your host comes, he will say to you, 'Friend, move up to a better place.' Then you will be honored in the presence of all your fellow guests."

This parable has many applications, but when applied to the workplace, the issue is self-exaltation versus humility. The elites in the story scrambled for the place of honor but they were moved to a lower place by the host. The host in this parable represents God. It is God who will move you, the humble person, to a better place where you will be honored in the presence of all your fellow guests.

Self-exaltation will always backfire. Its ultimate fruit is humiliation at the hand of God, but the humble person will be honored by God and others.

Luke 14:11 expresses Jesus's key point: "For everyone who exalts himself will be humbled, and he who humbles himself will be exalted."

Cultivate a lifestyle of humility and make it a part of your witness to others. Use your talents and pursue success while avoiding the worldly practice of self-exaltation. Titus 3:2 instructs you to "show true humility toward all men."

To be humble is to be like your Savior, Jesus Christ.

80

THE SILENT CHRISTIAN

MANY OF US hesitate at the thought of mentioning Jesus Christ to a coworker. We become like Peter in Mark 14:38 (NASB) when Jesus says to him, "The spirit is willing, but the flesh is weak."

Why do we remain silent about Christ at those times when the Holy Spirit is telling us to speak?

Jesus clearly wants us to spread the Good News. Matthew 28:19 says, "Therefore go and make disciples of all nations." Mark 16:15 says, "Go into all the world and preach the good news." And Acts 1:8 says, "Be my witnesses…to the ends of the earth."

The workplace is where you mingle with the nations and the world on a regular basis, and there are occasions when it would be appropriate to speak of Jesus Christ and his Word.

In addition, here in the United States, federal law gives you the freedom to discuss matters of faith at work. Religious speech is a protected workplace right under Title VII of the Civil Rights Act of 1964. As Christians we can talk about Jesus in the workplace just as openly as we would sports, politics, or the latest TV show. If all this is true, and it is, why do we hesitate?

The answer for many of us is found in John 12:42–43:

> Yet at the same time many even among the leaders believed in him. But because of the Pharisees they would not confess their faith for fear they would be put out of the synagogue; for they loved praise from men more than praise from God.

This passage reveals two reasons why we choose to be silent before others.

Fear of what others may think

John 12:42 says, "They would not confess their faith for fear they would be put out of the synagogue." The "they" in this verse are believers who feared rejection by their peer group. Their fear of rejection stifled their speech.

Proverbs 29:25 declares, "Fear of man will prove to be a snare." Fear of mentioning Jesus Christ in a conversation with others is a spiritual snare that holds you against your will. Jesus is the opposite of a snare—he is freedom personified.

Galatians 5:1 says, "It is for freedom that Christ has set us free," and 2 Corinthians 3:17 says, "Where the Spirit of the Lord is, there is freedom."

Simply telling a workplace friend how Jesus Christ changed your life for the better is nothing to be feared.

A love for the praise from men

John 12:43 reveals another reason why we remain silent, which is that we love the "praise from men more than praise from God." The NASB translates this verse as, "For they loved the approval of men rather than the approval of God."

Being needy for the world's praise and approval can keep you silent concerning the greatness of God. In the context of John 12:43, seeking the approval of men is spiritual submission to the wrong master.

Paul says in 1 Corinthians 1:18–19, "For the message of the cross is foolishness to those who are perishing, but to us who are being saved it is the power of God."

🌿 Jesus Christ is the best news on the planet.

81

SALT AND LIGHT IN THE WORKPLACE

J ESUS LIVED, WORKED, and ministered in the world; and he calls you to do the same.

The workplace is your mission field.

After the Last Supper, Jesus was reflecting on his ministry with the disciples when he said in John 16:28, "I came from the Father and entered the world."

Later, when praying to his Father, Jesus went further and included us in his prayer. Jesus says in John 17:15, "My prayer is not that you take them out of the world." He wants us in the world just like he was in the world.

Jesus spent most of his earthly ministry in what we would refer to as the streets. He was a marketplace minister. Jesus made daily contact with all sorts and conditions of mankind.

Two gospel passages make this clear. Matthew 9:10 states, "While Jesus was having dinner at Matthew's house, many tax collectors and 'sinners' came and ate with him," and Luke 15:1 states, "Now the tax collectors and 'sinners' were all gathering around to hear him."

Jesus still has work to do here and now, and his method is to do it through us, his church. As a Christian who goes to a job five days a week, you are Christ's representative at your place of employment. The workplace is most definitely in the world, and it is your mission field. It is within commuting distance from your home, and you are there five days a week.

Be salt and light to others.

Be a witness to your coworkers by simply being God's salt and light to them.

In the first verses of Matthew 5, which is part of the Sermon on the Mount, Jesus describes what Christians are like, and later in the same chapter, Matthew 5:13–14, Jesus describes what Christians do. This is where he declares, "You are the salt of the earth...You are the light of the world."

As a Christian you are salt, which means you inhibit decay and add flavor. You are light, which means you dispel the darkness and illuminate the way so others can see. These two metaphors describe the basics of your evangelistic ministry in the workplace.

Your salt and light can be seen and experienced by others. It is on display every hour of every day. God has already transformed you, and he is ready to transform those around you.

Notice in Matthew 5 that Jesus did not give you "Six Steps to Evangelizing Your Coworkers" or anything similar. There are no presentations to memorize, nor is a degree in theology required—just manifest the character of Jesus Christ and love people the same way he loves people.

🌿 You are God's salt and light to your coworkers.

SUMMARY OF PART SIX

Work as Ministry

Key Principles

71. Work as Ministry: Working Christians are ministers of the Gospel at their places of employment. The true value of your work is not a matter of just dollars and cents.

72. Your Work is Your Witness: Witness to your coworkers through your exemplary work ethic and excellent job performance. Your good work will exalt Christ and his teachings.

73. Lessons from Paul's Conversion: Jesus was a marketplace minister and so are you. Don't give up on the lost in your midst. Any person can receive Jesus Christ anywhere, anytime, and in any circumstance. No one is beyond his reach.

74. Bringing Good News to Work: All Christians are evangelists, and our ministry in the workplace is not to condemn our coworkers, but to bring the good news and glad tidings of Jesus Christ.

75. Serving God Full Time: You do not have to quit your job in order to serve God because you are already serving him full time with, and through, your career. Do you want to change the world for Jesus Christ? Then start with the people who are in the place where you spend most of your time—your workplace.

76. Peter's Transformation: God transformed Peter, and he can do the same for you. Like Peter God can accomplish great things through you regardless of your background or personal struggles.

77. Bringing God to Work: The centrality of Christ encompasses all things, and this includes your daily labor. Bringing God to work is the best career decision you will ever make.

78. Good Works in the Workplace: As Christians we don't do good works to *get* saved—we do good works *because* we are saved. Doing good works for others is the fruit of your salvation in Jesus Christ, and it is an important part of your Christian witness to your coworkers.

79. Humility in the Workplace: Biblical humility is simply recognizing your dependence on God. Humility exalts God, while pride, the opposite of humility, exalts self. To be humble is to be like your Savior, Jesus Christ.

80. The Silent Christian: Telling a workplace friend how Jesus Christ changed your life for the better is nothing to be feared. Jesus is the best news on the planet. Getting along with others in the workplace does not have to be at the expense of your Christian faith.

81. Salt and Light in the Workplace: Jesus lived, worked, and ministered in the world, and he calls you to do the same. The workplace is the ripest of mission fields. It is within commuting distance from your home, and you are there five days a week.

Key Verses

Proverbs 22:4: Humility and the fear of the Lord bring wealth and honor and life.

Matthew 5:13–14: "You are the salt of the earth…You are the light of the world."

Mark 16:15: He said to them, "Go into all the world and preach the good news to all creation."

Luke 2:52: And Jesus grew in wisdom and stature, and in favor with God and men.

Luke 4:18–19: "The Spirit of the Lord is on me, because he has anointed me to preach good news to the poor. He has sent me to proclaim freedom for the prisoners and recovery of sight for the blind, to release the oppressed, to proclaim the year of the Lord's favor."

Luke 14:7–10: When he noticed how the guests picked the places of honor at the table, he told them this parable: "When someone invites you to a wedding feast, do not take the place of honor, for a person more distinguished than you may have been invited. If so, the host who invited both of you will come and say to you, 'Give this man your seat.' Then, humiliated, you will have to take the least important place. But when you are invited, take the lowest place, so that when your host comes, he will say to you, 'Friend, move up to a better place.' Then you will be honored in the presence of all your fellow guests."

Luke 14:11: "For everyone who exalts himself will be humbled, and he who humbles himself will be exalted."

John 12:42–43: Yet at the same time many even among the leaders believed in him. But because of the Pharisees they would not confess their faith for fear they would be put out of the synagogue; for they loved praise from men more than praise from God.

John 17:15a: "My prayer is not that you take them out of the world."

Acts 2:41: Those who accepted his message were baptized, and about three thousand were added to their number that day.

Acts 9:20: At once he began to preach in the synagogues that Jesus is the Son of God.

Romans 10:15b: How beautiful are the feet of those who bring good news!

2 Corinthians 5:18–20a: All this is from God, who reconciled us to himself through Christ and gave us the ministry of reconciliation: that God was reconciling the world to himself in Christ, not counting men's sins against them. And he has committed to us the message of reconciliation. We are therefore Christ's ambassadors, as though God were making his appeal through us.

Ephesians 2:10: For we are God's workmanship, created in Christ Jesus to do good works, which God prepared in advance for us to do.

Titus 2:9–10: Teach slaves to be subject to their masters in everything, to try to please them, not to talk back to them, and not to steal from them, but to show that they can be fully trusted, so that in every way they will make the teaching about God our Savior attractive.

James 4:10: Humble yourselves before the Lord, and he will lift you up.

1 Peter 2:9: A chosen people, a royal priesthood, a holy nation, a people belonging to God, that you may declare the praises of him who called you out of darkness into his wonderful light.

FOCUS QUESTIONS

Are there times in your workday when it would be easy to compromise God's Word? How do you handle these temptations?

What aspects of your job require you to provide services to others? How does your salvation in Christ affect the way you provide these services?

Read Titus 2:9–10. Is your work ethic making Christ attractive to others? Are there some things you need to do to improve your job performance?

Read Luke 4:18–19. Give examples of the freedom, recovery, and release that Jesus has brought into your life. How can you share this good news with others?

Do you see yourself as a minister of the Gospel of Jesus Christ in the workplace? Why or why not?

How has Jesus Christ changed your life for the better? In what ways is he now using you to advance his Kingdom in the workplace?

Think of one or more of your favorite verses. Give examples of the truth of God's Word being demonstrated in your life right now.

Read Ephesians 2:10. What are some good works you can do for others at your place of employment? How does it feel when someone does a good work for you, and vice versa?

Read Numbers 12:3. What is the connection between Moses's great success in life and the fact that he was "more humble than anyone else on the face of the earth"?

At one time or another, all of us have remained silent about our faith when we knew God wanted us to speak. What can you do to overcome this fear of speaking out?

In what ways is the workplace the ripest of mission fields?

What does it mean to be salt and light to your coworkers?

CONCLUSION

THERE IS NO better career guide for the workplace Christian than the Bible. Billions have been printed or downloaded—it is the bestselling book of all time.

The Bible is a God-inspired classic and every word of it is true. Isaiah 40:8 declares, "The grass withers and the flowers fall, but the word of our God stands forever."

What does the Bible say about your work?

Your work is a high calling from God, and it is good. Christians should be the best workers in every organization.

Work is more than a paycheck and more than mere secular labor—it's the fulfillment of God's creation mandate to mankind. God designed you to engage with his creation—to be active, productive, and creative. All human work has a spiritual component.

At its core your work is a service to God to be performed to his glory. Do great work regardless of its pay or prestige.

Affirm the good work of others in your family, workplace, and community. In God's eyes no job is too small.

Work performed under God's governance will always pay off. He intends for the impact of your labor to be wide-spread and long-lasting. Honor God with your career success.

Even Jesus learned a trade and worked with his hands. He was a craftsman. If any person could have been exempted from daily labor it would have been him. Yet Jesus worked in his community like the rest of us, and in doing this he validated the significance and dignity of everyday, ordinary work. When you get up and go to work you are following in the footsteps of your Savior, Jesus Christ.

Work isn't easy and workplace trials are inevitable. These trials are the consequence of living and working in our fallen world. God promises you, the Christian, that he can bring good out of every on-the-job trial you will ever experience. God is always for you and never against you.

God put boundaries on your work and he did it for your own good. Work has limits. Enjoy regular times of rest, celebration, play, and leisure. Spend part of your retirement years helping the next generation.

Bringing God to work is the best career decision you will ever make. Work changes, but God never does.

You are a full-time minister of the Gospel of Jesus Christ at your place of employment.

Remember Psalm 128:1–2: "Blessed are all who fear the Lord, who walk in his ways. You will eat the fruit of your labor; blessings and prosperity will be yours."

APPENDIX

STUDY GUIDE

Start a *God's Career Guide* discussion group with other like-minded Christians at your place of employment, your church, your home, or in your community. As fellow believers we are called to equip, edify, and strengthen each other.

Study Group Guidelines

The format of *God's Career Guide* is well-suited for small-group discussion.

- **Select an overall leader** with the responsibility of leading each session or theme series (see Discussion Themes). Or rotate this responsibility with different leaders for each week.
- **Use the key principles, key verses, and focus questions** at the end of parts 1 to 6 of the book to facilitate the discussion.
- **Focus on one or more** God's Career Guide **lessons** per week.

- **Stay on topic.** Make sure everyone gets a chance to contribute, and do not let one person dominate the conversation.
- **Respect each other's time**. Preread the assigned lessons and come prepared to contribute to the meetings. Begin and end the sessions at the agreed upon times.
- **Honor the confidentiality** of what is shared in the group.
- **Be an open group** and invite others to attend.
- **Ask for personal testimonies** on how God is changing the lives of your group members for the better.
- **Pray** for each other.

Verses to Remember

Apply Jesus's words in Matthew 18:20 when he declares, "For where two or three come together in my name, there am I with them."

The writer of Hebrews 10:25 says, "Let us not give up meeting together, as some are in the habit of doing, but let us encourage one another."

Paul is speaking to the church in 1 Corinthians 10:31: "Whatever you do, do it all for the glory of God."

Discussion Themes

Select a discussion theme from the list below.

Discuss the lessons in the order presented within the theme rather than in the order they appear in the book. Depending on the number of lessons involved, a theme may be discussed in just one session or over a series of two or more sessions.

The following are recommended *God's Career Guide* discussion themes

- **Be an Encourager:** The Spirit of Edification (p. 156), Encourage One Another (p. 149), and Bringing Good News to Work (p. 248)
- **Blessings:** The Keys to God's Blessings (p. 125), Five Conditional Blessings (p. 93), The Blessed Life (p. 122), The Secret of Being Content (p. 113), and All Hard Work Brings a Profit (p. 86)
- **Book Categories:** Select one or more lessons per week from each *God's Career Guide* category beginning with part 1 (Biblical Principles of Work). Advance to part 2 (Workplace Trials) the next week, then to part 3 (Favor and Blessings) until all of the six

categories have been discussed at least once. Return to part 1 and repeat the cycle until every lesson has been addressed.

- **Choices:** Choosing Righteousness (p. 88) and The Yielded Life (p. 214)
- **Companions:** Sluggards Don't Work (p. 21), Dealing with a Fool (p. 146), Walk with the Wise (p. 140), and Church and Work (p. 162)
- **Decision Making:** Freedom Within Limits (p. 208) and Decision Making God's Way (p. 225)
- **Evangelism:** Salt and Light in the Workplace (p. 267), Your Work is Your Witness (p. 242), Good Works in the Workplace (p. 258), and The Silent Christian (p. 264)
- **Faith in Action:** Joseph: From Slave to Ruler (p. 53), Ruth: a Blessed Laborer (p. 99), Joshua's Early Training (p. 216), and Jonathan's Faith (p. 219)
- **Freestyle:** Have a different discussion leader each week, and the various leaders can choose the lessons for their assigned week.
- **Giving to Others:** The Generous Worker (p. 154) and Working to Give (p. 169)
- **Humility Versus Pride:** Humility in the Workplace (p. 261) and The Problem with Self-Esteem (p. 227)
- **Jesus the Carpenter:** Why Was Jesus a Carpenter? (p. 33), Jesus's Ordinary Work (p. 12), and Bringing God to Work (p. 256)
- **Leadership:** Deborah's Leadership (p. 151), Jehoshaphat's Praise (p. 107), Moses's Great Decision (p. 116), The Servant Leader (p. 177), and The Leader Who Empowers (p. 171)

- **Trials, the Upside:** God and Your Career Trials (p. 47), How to Build Character (p. 56), Four Keys to Effective Prayer (p. 58), Trials as Training (p. 72), and Find Strength in the Lord (p. 74)

A MESSAGE FROM
PATRICK LAYHEE

GREETINGS AND THANK you for your interest in *God's Career Guide*. As one workplace Christian to another, I wish you the best in your career.

I have been studying, teaching, and writing about the Bible since receiving Jesus Christ in 1985. In 2008 I began to focus my teaching efforts on the topic of Christianity in the workplace. Subsequently, I moved my ministry from the local church classroom to the broader Christian community. GodsCareerGuide. com went online in 2009, and this book was published in 2013.

In my professional life, I have earned two college degrees and worked almost exclusively in the recruiting and staffing industry. I have been a self-employed recruiter; CEO of a large urban staffing firm; and VP of a national, publicly traded staffing company. I am currently the owner of a small professional recruiting firm in Sugar Land, Texas, a suburb of Houston.

My favorite Old Testament verse is Proverbs 9:10: "The fear of the Lord is the beginning of wisdom, and knowledge of the Holy One is understanding." My favorite New Testament verse is 2 Corinthians 3:17: "Now the Lord is the Spirit, and where the Spirit of the Lord is, there is freedom."

My wife, Nalani, and I met in Hawaii while we were both attending high school there. We have three children and five grandchildren.

Feel free to share your thoughts regarding *God's Career Guide*. I would like to hear from you. E-mail me through the GodsCareerGuide.com web site or send your letter to PO Box 16115, Sugar Land, TX 77496-6115.

Sincerely,
Patrick Layhee

RESOURCES

Friesen, Garry with Maxson, J. Robin, *Decision Making and the Will of God*, Multnomah Books, 1980, 2004

King Jr., Martin Luther, *Strength to Love,* Fortress Press, 1963, 2010

Miller, David W., *God at Work: The History and Promise of the Faith at Work Movement.* Oxford University Press, 2007

Murray, Andrew, *Humility*, Bridge-Logos Publishers, 2000

Materials from Biblesoft, Inc.:

PC Bible Study V5.0, Biblesoft, Inc. © 1988–2007

Biblesoft's *New Exhaustive Strong's Numbers and Concordance with Expanded Greek-Hebrew Dictionary*, Copyright © 1994, 2003, 2006 Biblesoft, Inc. and International Bible Translators, Inc.

Englishman's Concordance, Electronic Database, Copyright (c) 1993 by Biblesoft, Inc.

Interlinear Transliterated Bible, Copyright © 1994, 2003, 2006 by Biblesoft, Inc.

International Standard Bible Encyclopaedia, Copyright © 1995-1996, 2003 by Biblesoft, Inc.

Keil & Delitzsch Commentary on the Old Testament, Copyright © 1996 by Hendrickson Publishers, Inc., New Updated Edition

New Exhaustive Strong's Numbers and Concordance with Expanded Greek-Hebrew Dictionary by Biblesoft, Inc. and International Bible Translators, Inc. © 1985 by William B. Eerdmans Publishing Company

Robertson's Word Pictures in the New Testament, Electronic Database, Copyright © 1997, 2003, 2005, 2006 by Biblesoft, Inc.

The Biblical Illustrator, Electronic Database, Copyright © 2002, 2003, 2006 Ages Software, Inc. and Biblesoft, Inc.

The New Unger's Bible Dictionary, Original Work Copyright © 1957, Revised Editions Copyright © 1961

Treasury of Scripture Knowledge, Electronic Database. Copyright (c) 1993 by Biblesoft, Inc.

Theological Dictionary of the New Testament, Copyright (c) 1985, William B. Eerdmans Publishing Company, Grand Rapids, Michigan

NOTES

NOTES

NOTES

30403624R00171

Made in the USA
San Bernardino, CA
12 February 2016